REVELATION BIBLE STUDY

DISCOVER PRACTICAL INSIGHTS FROM JOHN'S EPIC VISION

40-DAY BIBLE STUDY SERIES
BOOK 8

PETER DEHAAN

Revelation Bible Study: Discover 40 Practical Insights from John's Epic Vision (Originally published as *A New Heaven and a New Earth*)

Copyright © 2022, 2025 by Peter DeHaan.

40-Day Bible Study Series, Book 8

Unless otherwise noted, Scriptures taken from the Holy Bible, New International Version®, NIV®. Copyright © 1973, 1978, 1984, 2011 by Biblica, Inc.™ Used by permission of Zondervan. All rights reserved worldwide. www.zondervan.com The "NIV" and "New International Version" are trademarks registered in the United States Patent and Trademark Office by Biblica, Inc.™

Library of Congress Control Number: 2024923137

Published by Rock Rooster Books, Grand Rapids, Michigan

ISBN:

- 979-8-88809-117-3 (e-book)
- 979-8-88809-118-0 (paperback)
- 979-8-88809-119-7 (hardcover)
- 979-8-88809-120-3 (audiobook)

Credits:

- Developmental editor: Kathryn Wilmotte
- Copy editor/proofreader: Robyn Mulder
- Cover design: Fanderclai Design
- Author photo: Chelsie Jensen Photography

To Chris Alexander

Series by Peter DeHaan

40-Day Bible Study Series takes a fresh and practical look into Scripture, book by book.

Bible Character Sketches Series celebrates people in Scripture, from the well-known to the obscure.

Holiday Celebration Bible Study Series rejoices in the holidays with Jesus.

Visiting Churches Series takes an in-person look at church practices and traditions to inform and inspire today's followers of Jesus.

Be the first to hear about Peter's new books and receive updates at PeterDeHaan.com/updates.

CONTENTS

THE BOOK OF REVELATION

When I ask people what book of the Bible they'd like to understand better, the most frequent response is Revelation. I get that. John's future-focused vision recorded in the book of Revelation overflows with evocative imagery that sparks our imagination even as we struggle to make sense of it.

Revelation is an intriguing prophecy, full of fascinating allusions, overflowing with enigma. What does it mean? When will it happen?

Many people have invested time—perhaps too much time—attempting to interpret the uncertainty of John's epic vision. Even with their best work, it's as if we see into the mirror dimly (1 Corinthians 13:12).

Additionally, each person who tries to explain this vision often piles on additional complexity to an already complicated narrative. Too often, I fear, in a pursuit of clarity they end up connecting dots that may not relate.

We should not strive to make Revelation into something it's not. It's not a precise cipher detailing what will happen in the future. We also shouldn't try to link John's compelling narrative with real people, places, or events. Instead, we should understand Revelation as the glorious mystery it is, embracing one essential, concluding idea: In the end God will prevail, vanquishing the enemy permanently and living for eternity with his purified bride, the Church of Jesus.

The goal of this book is to take a fresh approach. Read on to find out what to expect and what not to expect in this book. As you move forward, my prayer is that you will walk away with practical and understandable insights that you can apply to your life and spiritual journey today.

To begin, let's consider the three basic options we could take to explore the book of Revelation.

A Future Look

The apostle John's vision as recorded in the book of Revelation is a future-focused glimpse into what will one day be. The most common investigation into Revelation examines this prophetic future and attempts to explain it.

If you're someone who wants a detailed treatise on what the end times will look like, I'm about to disappoint you.

Here is the essential summary, the key takeaway concerning the future, from the book of Revelation:

At the end of time, we will see an epic battle between good and evil.

God wins.

The end.

The details don't matter to us today. Not really. Here's why.

First, let's consider prophecies in the Old Testament, which anticipated Jesus, the coming Messiah who would save God's people. Though today we can read the Old Testament text with clarity and understand what the prophecies predicted, most people in Jesus's day got it wrong. Even his disciples were slow to catch on (Luke 24:25).

Two thousand years ago, most everyone's understanding of the prophets was to expect a military savior who would free the people from the tyranny of an oppressing ruling nation (John 12:13). Few people expected a spiritual savior who would free them from the tyranny of sin (Matthew 1:21 and 1 Timothy 1:15).

The people of that day had much less information to deal with than we do now, whereas we have a multitude of narratives and conflicting views constantly bombarding us. If they were confused then—in a simpler time—how much more likely are we to face confusion and make a wrong assessment of John's New Testament prophecy?

Next, Jesus says that no one will know when the end will happen. Yet many attempt to use Revelation as a primer to unlock the code that will reveal exactly what Jesus said is unknown (Matthew 24:36, Mark 13:32, and Revelation 3:3). Paul and Peter agree with Jesus (1 Thessalonians 5:1–3 and 2 Peter 3:10).

Third, many people think we're currently living

in the last times and that the end is near. Yet Jesus's followers thought the same thing two millennia ago (1 Peter 4:7). Every generation, I suspect, has voiced this same perspective ever since. As such, I don't think the end is near. I don't expect to be around for these end time events (Matthew 24:6, Mark 13:7, and Luke 21:9).

Last, even if we did correctly interpret John's vision of what will be, what difference would it make? What will happen will happen. And if we are here when it happens, there's nothing we can do about it but remain faithful to Jesus and seek his strength to stand up under what will occur at that time.

A Past Look

The second basic approach to take in understanding the book of Revelation is to apply its narrative to the culture of that day. That is to take John's imagery from his vision and connect it with the events from the perspective of life 2,000 years ago.

Though this makes for a most interesting excursion, what effect would this new knowledge have on how we live our life today? Though we'd know more, we'd only be amassing knowledge and not informing our actions and our attitudes to affect our faith journey. Jesus wants changed hearts, not changed minds.

Another weakness of this approach is that we must rely on historical accounts of the past to enlighten us on that day's correlation with the imagery of John's vision. The items we connect will be only as accurate as the version of history we choose to consider. Just as historical accounts disagree, any conclusions we make would diverge.

To put this in a more practical perspective, how often have we heard a preacher explain the historical context surrounding a passage of Scripture? The explanation illuminates our understanding (our knowledge), but later another teacher offers a different—and sometimes conflicting—historical perspective. Therefore, connecting Scripture with history is only as valuable as the accuracy of the historical account we follow.

This effort can produce a most intellectually satisfying result, but we can expect little more from it.

A Present Look

The third approach we can take to the book of Revelation is to explore the ways that we can apply it to our lives today. Though taking a future look or a past glance have their intellectual rewards, we can benefit most by seeking how Revelation can best inform what we do, think, and believe today.

That's the goal of this book.

In doing so, we will not ignore the essential future-focused message and the hope it provides, but we will do so only to the extent that it illuminates our understanding today.

What do you think about the concise, three-line summary of the book of Revelation? How willing are you to look at the book of Revelation from a fresh perspective?

[Discover more about how to embrace the book of Revelation in 2 Timothy 3:16.]

DAY 1: THE REVELATION OF JESUS
REVELATION 1:1–3

The revelation from Jesus Christ, which God gave him to show his servants what must soon take place. (Revelation 1:1)

We think of the book of Revelation as John's revelation, but, in fact, it is Jesus's. John is only the recipient. This revelation comes from Jesus. Father God gave it to him. Jesus shares this revelation with John through a supernatural vision as the apostle communes with God in the spiritual realm (Revelation 1:10).

An angel shows up in John's vision to reveal Jesus's revelation. The intent of the vision—that is, the revelation—is to show John what will soon take place.

As we comprehend time, we can easily conclude that *soon* has already occurred, since we are now 2,000 years distant from John's recording of these words. Yet we must acknowledge that God views time differently than we do. A thousand years to us are but a day to him and a day to us may be a thousand years to him (Psalm 90:4 and 2 Peter 3:8).

So when we read John's words that the time is near, this shouldn't perplex us. If we literally equate 2,000 years of our time to two days for God, then we are but two days removed from this revelation. In this respect, we can accept that the time is, indeed, quite near.

Yet a literal application of Scripture's statement about God's view of time may be an overreach. The principle to grasp, however, is that we comprehend time much differently than God. Given this, we can accept that these events will soon take place because the time is near, even though those words took place two millennia ago. Time isn't a problem for God, only for us.

John confirms that his vision is a prophecy. In a delightful simplicity, we'll receive God's blessing by merely reading it, hearing it, and taking it to heart (Revelation 1:3). Don't miss this point.

John doesn't say we need to understand what it says. Just like the rest of Scripture, we can now only know in part. Rather, we should read it and be amazed. That's the intent. And God will bless us when we do.

Beyond that we find another hint at the purpose of John's vision much later in Revelation. The aim of Revelation may be simply to worship God and celebrate Jesus (Revelation 19:10).

How well do we accept that we understand time differently than God? How content are we to read, hear, and take to heart the book of Revelation?

[Discover what else John says about Jesus and how it relates to our view of time in John 1:1–5.]

DAY 2: THE ALPHA AND THE OMEGA
REVELATION 1:4–8

"I am the Alpha and the Omega," says the Lord God, *"who is, and who was, and who is to come, the Almighty."*
(Revelation 1:8)

Having worked our way through John's short prologue to his book, we move forward with excitement about what we'll encounter next. When we realize, however, that the next passage is only a greeting, we're tempted to skim by it and get to the good stuff.

But we shouldn't do that. Slow down. John packs much into these four verses, and we don't want to miss what he has to say.

John addresses his writing to the seven churches in Asia (and we'll soon learn who they are and more about them). To these churches John proclaims grace and peace. This blessing comes from eternal Father God who exists in time present, time past, and time future as someone who is, was, and is to come. Also implied as a sender is the Holy Spirit in the form of the sevenfold Spirit who resides in heaven. Jesus, as part of the Trinity, exists as a third sender of this message to the seven churches.

John then gives us three characteristics of Jesus. He is the faithful witness. He is the firstborn from the dead. He is ruler over the kings of the earth. Each one of these traits deserves deep contemplation.

Furthermore, Jesus loves us. He showed his deep, unsurpassed love for us when he died as the ultimate sacrifice to free us from the punishment that our sins (the times when we missed the mark) deserve, according to the Old Testament law.

By doing so he makes us into his kingdom, the kingdom of God.

We see in the Bible's four biographies of Jesus (Matthew, Mark, Luke, and John) that he says much about the kingdom of God (synonymous with the kingdom of heaven, as Matthew renders it). Jesus teaches often on the kingdom of God, whereas he only uses the word *church* twice. We will do well to study what Jesus says about the kingdom of God and use it to inform our perspective and guide our relationship with him.

Not only does Jesus make us into his kingdom, but he also makes us his priests. Every one of us who follows him as our Savior is a priest. Our lineage doesn't matter, as it did in the Old Testament. We also don't need an advanced education, as our religious institutions require today, or special training. To be Jesus's priest, we just need to follow him. It's that simple.

And as his priest our duty is to serve God.

We can do all this because Jesus is the Alpha and the Omega, the first and the last. He is the Almighty who exists from eternity past into eternity future.

Do we view ourselves as part of Jesus's kingdom, the kingdom of God? Are we willing to accept our standing as Jesus's priests and act accordingly?

[Discover more about the kingdom of God in Mark 1:15 and Luke 16:16. Read about us being priests in 1 Peter 2:4–9.]

DAY 3: DO NOT BE AFRAID
REVELATION 1:9–20

When I saw him, I fell at his feet as though dead. Then he placed his right hand on me and said: "Do not be afraid."
(Revelation 1:17)

The apostle John, exiled on the island of Patmos for telling others about Jesus, connects with God on a spiritual level, not the physical realm but the supernatural. This occurs on the Lord's Day. We could assume that the Lord's Day is a reference to Sunday, or perhaps the Sabbath. Or it might be another special day of celebration.

Since "the Lord's Day" doesn't occur anywhere

else in the Bible, we can't use Scripture to inform our understanding of what it means. Or maybe we can. The phrase "the day of the Lord" does appear throughout the Bible, and it references the end of our present age. Perhaps that's the vantage of John's vision, as if speaking back to us today from the end of time.

Regardless, John hears someone speaking. It's Jesus, commanding him—with a loud voice like a trumpet—to record his vision and send it to seven churches, which we'll learn more about in Revelation 2 and 3.

John turns to the sound and sees seven golden lampstands and someone who is "like a son of man." (See Daniel 7:13.) John later confirms that this son of man is none other than Jesus.

The description of our Savior fills us with awe: a golden sash, head and hair as white as snow, and eyes blazing like fire. He has feet of glowing bronze and a voice roaring like rushing waters. He holds seven stars in his hand. From his mouth comes a double-edged sword. We may see this imagery as representing the spoken word of God, the sword of the Spirit (Ephesians 6:17). Last, Jesus's face shines with the brilliance of the sun.

John takes this in and falls at Jesus's feet.

It may be that John is simply in awe of Jesus or that he is experiencing a paralyzing terror. It might be both. Regardless, John lies there as if dead.

Then Jesus does the most amazing thing to comfort his overwrought disciple. He places his hand on John and says, "Do not be afraid."

What a relief. We can feel the tension release from John's body—and from ours as we live vicariously through the apostle's experience.

Having gotten John's attention, and ours, Jesus again confirms he is the first and last. He is the living one. Though once dead—when he died for us —he is now alive for all eternity. He has power over death and hell. How comforting. How reassuring for those of us who follow him.

He tells John to record his vision of what is and what will be. Then he gives us a key to guide our understanding of the vision: the seven stars that he holds in his hand are angels, his messengers to the seven churches. And the seven lampstands represent the seven churches themselves. This explanation will help us better understand the next two chapters of the book of Revelation.

When in Jesus's presence, will we fall at his feet in awe or in terror? Will he need to tell us not to be afraid?

[Discover more about another time when people fall at the feet of the resurrected Jesus in Matthew 28:9–10.]

BONUS CONTENT: WHAT IS AND WHAT WILL BE

"Write, therefore, what you have seen, what is now and what will take place later." (Revelation 1:19)

John records Jesus's own words when he says that the vision John is about to receive will address what is (the present) and what will take place later (the future). Therefore, as we move forward, we can consider Revelation in three sections:

The Foundation (Revelation 1)

In addition to setting the basis for the rest of the book, chapter 1 is inspiring in that it hints at what our relationship with God can be like when we connect with him in the spiritual realm. We should not consider this unique to John and should embrace it as available to us through the Holy Spirit that God sends to everyone who follows Jesus.

Messages to the Seven Churches (Revelation 2–3)

The letters to the seven churches address their specific situations two millennia ago, which speak to *their* present but reside in *our* past. While we can receive encouragement from their successes and learn from their failures, we need to remember that they're the primary audience and we are the secondary one, as is the case with all the other letters in the New Testament.

We must acknowledge that these words are to the seven churches and not to us. Though we can learn from these letters, we are not the main recipients and must take care to not make these messages into more than God intends.

God shares words of commendation and condemnation. We'll do well to carefully consider what he says. Though this relates directly to those seven specific churches, the broader application can inform our church today.

What can we learn from these churches to affirm and reform our local branch of Jesus's church now? First, we must celebrate what we do well, without a smug sense of pride and with an eye toward maintaining and developing each strength.

More importantly, we must ask if any of Jesus's criticism for those churches rightly apply to us in the present. If we're willing to read with an open mind, we will find much to correct, as well as warnings of what to avoid.

As we read the seven letters, let's relish the rhythmic repetition of their format, look for patterns in each text, and consider the differences between the passages. Take note that these are the words of Jesus.

Prophecy (Revelation 4–22)

The rest of the book of Revelation looks forward to the future. Throughout these final nineteen chapters, the intent is not for us to discern when these events will occur. Recall that Jesus says no one knows the time and date of when the end will happen except for the Father. There is no secret timetable for us to decode.

Instead, we can celebrate three key realities as we read the words in Revelation. First, God is awesome and worthy of our worship. Second, Jesus is powerful. And last, those whose names appear in the book of life will have a glorious future stretching into eternity.

We'll see these truths unfold more fully as we read the last two chapters of Revelation. Through them we can be in awe of Almighty God, even if we can't completely understand what the details of John's vision mean and how to perceive the supernatural imagery.

Are we content to allow John's vision to bring us into a deeper worship of Father God and a celebration of Jesus? What must we adjust in our perspective of the book of Revelation to do so?

[Discover more about when the end will occur in Matthew 24:36 and Mark 13:32.]

DAY 4: THE CHURCH IN EPHESUS: THEIR FIRST LOVE

REVELATION 2:1–7

"You have forsaken the love you had at first." (Revelation 2:4)

Of the seven churches, we know most about the church in Ephesus because of the letter Paul wrote to them (the book of Ephesians). In this epistle Paul teaches them about three main topics: Jesus's church, faithfulness, and their relationships with each other. We can assume this content is in answer to questions they asked or in response to issues that had come to Paul's attention.

We can view Jesus's letter to the Ephesians in Revelation as a follow up to Paul's. In it, Jesus affirms the Ephesians' many admirable characteristics, including their virtuous deeds, diligent work, and perseverance. They have not tolerated false teachers, have persevered under hardship, and have remained strong. They also stand against the practice of the Nicolaitans. We don't know much about the Nicolaitans. With only two biblical mentions, both in the book of Revelation, we do, however, know that God doesn't like their practices, and that's what matters.

Sandwiched within this affirming list of positive characteristics is one criticism for the church in Ephesus. It is, nonetheless, a weighty one. They have forsaken the love they had at first.

Though they once loved Jesus, their passion for him has faded over time to the point where they've now forgotten it. Yes, they're living out their faith in many positive ways, but they lost sight of why they're doing what they're doing. They've forsaken their love for their Savior.

Jesus loved them—and he loves us—so much that he died for all their mistakes—and all of ours. This is the ultimate expression of love, to die for someone else who's unworthy of such a grand sacrifice.

As recipients of Jesus's love, we love him in

return. He deserves it. We can show our love for him through our worship. We can also show our love for him through our attitudes and our actions by what we say, by what we think, and by what we do.

May we never abandon our love for Jesus. May we walk in his love and keep ourselves in it throughout our entire lives.

Do we love Jesus now as much as we once did? What must we do to not forsake our love for Jesus?

[Discover more about dying for someone else in Romans 5:7. Read more about love in Luke 10:27, Ephesians 5:1–2, and Jude 1:20–21.]

BONUS CONTENT: RECURRING WORDS AND THEMES

"Whoever has ears, let them hear what the Spirit says to the churches." (Revelation 2:7)

As mentioned earlier, Jesus's letters to the seven churches carry several recurring themes and meaningful repetition. Here are some key words to watch for as you read the seven letters:

- repent
- victorious
- deeds

There is also one significant repeating phrase:

"Whoever has ears, let them hear what the Spirit says to the churches." This idea of ears that hear—or don't hear—is a recurring theme throughout Scripture, occurring over fifty times in nineteen books, most prominently in Revelation. As we read and study God's Word, we need to truly hear what it says.

Beyond this, look for recurring themes in these seven letters such as obedience, perseverance, encouragement, and love.

Are we willing to hear what the Spirit says to the churches? What do our deeds say about us?

[Discover more about listening to Jesus in Matthew 11:2–15, Matthew 13:3–43, Mark 4:21–23, and Luke 14:25–35.]

DAY 5: THE CHURCH IN SMYRNA: FEARLESS SUFFERING

REVELATION 2:8–11

"Do not be afraid of what you are about to suffer."
(Revelation 2:10)

Unlike the church in Ephesus, the Bible gives us no other information about the church in Smyrna outside of two references in Revelation. And, unlike the church in Ephesus and most of the other churches we'll soon read about, Jesus doesn't offer any correction to them. He merely affirms their strengths and encourages them for what is to come.

Despite living in poverty, Jesus reminds them that they are, in fact, rich. Though physically poor, they have spiritual wealth. Like them, we can also have spiritual riches in Jesus and through Jesus.

In addition to seeing their physical poverty, Jesus also sees their afflictions. In the name of religion, others slander them. These slurs come from people who say they're Jews but aren't. Instead, they align with and worship Satan.

Amid the poverty and afflictions of their situation, Jesus offers the church reassurance. He tells them not to be afraid. This isn't in reference to the slander they're presently enduring, but a forward-looking encouragement to not fear the suffering they're about to encounter.

Jesus knows that the devil, Satan, will put their faith to the test. He'll stir up enemies to throw them in jail and persecute them, trying to get them to turn from their Savior. Some will face death.

Jesus encourages them to stand firm and remain committed to their faith. To those who persevere, he promises to give them the victor's crown, the crown of life.

We pray for God's blessings and often receive them, which happens more frequently than we deserve. But to expect that our walk with Jesus will always proceed smoothly and never encounter any problems isn't a realistic outlook. After all, he never said that following him would be easy.

Jesus said we'll face persecution. If we live for him, opposition from the world is inevitable—and unavoidable. Like the church in Smyrna, we, too, should not fear when we encounter suffering. We should be faithful, even under the threat of death. And when we stand firm in our faith, an eternal reward awaits us.

Are we spiritually rich in Jesus? Are we ready to stand firm in the face of persecution?

[Discover more about being spiritually rich in James 2:5 and the crown of life in James 1:12. Read about persecution in Mark 10:29–30.]

DAY 6: THE CHURCH IN PERGAMUM: REPENT

REVELATION 2:12–17

"Nevertheless, I have a few things against you."
(Revelation 2:14)

As with the church in Smyrna, the Bible tells us nothing more about the church in Pergamum. But like the church in Ephesus, Jesus's message to them offers both affirmation and correction.

Despite living where Satan has his stronghold, the church in Pergamum has remained true to Jesus. They have held on to their faith, even in the face of the martyrdom of Antipas. We join Jesus in commending them for standing firm.

Yet Jesus also has something against them, two key criticisms.

First, he denounces them for following the teaching of Balaam.

Balaam is an Old Testament character; God's people encounter him as they move to take the promised land.

When King Balak seeks a supernatural edge over the approaching Hebrew people, he sends elders from Moab and Midian for Balaam, a practitioner of divination, to proclaim curses against the Israelites.

God initially tells Balaam not to go and he doesn't. At the delegation's second request, however, God says for Balaam to go but to watch what he says, speaking only the words God gives him. Balaam obeys.

Yet in the end, God is not pleased with Balaam.

In the chapter following Balaam's story we read an epilogue of sorts. Moabite women are seducing the men of Israel to engage in sexually immoral behavior and offer sacrifices to their gods, eating the sacrificial meal and worshiping idols instead of God. Implicitly the people of Moab (and Midian) are following the advice of Balaam when they do this.

From this we can see that the teaching of Balaam relates to sexual immorality and worshiping other gods, represented by eating the meat sacrificed to these false gods.

Jesus's other criticism of the church in Pergamum is that they hold to the teaching of the Nicolaitans. We don't know what this teaching is, but we do know from Jesus's letter to the church in Ephesus that he hates their practices.

What is the solution for the church in Pergamum? To repent.

We often think of repenting as an initial turning from worldly behaviors to follow Jesus. But the context of repenting here applies to those who have already followed him.

Yes, Christians sometimes need to repent as well.

What do we need to repent from? Are there teachers we need to stop listening to because they're pulling us away from Jesus?

[Discover more about Balaam in Numbers 22–24, with an addendum in Numbers 25, along with

Numbers 31:16. Read what else the New Testament writers say about Balaam in 2 Peter 2:15 and Jude 1:11.]

DAY 7: THE CHURCH IN THYATIRA: SEXUAL IMMORALITY

REVELATION 2:18–29

"By her teaching she misleads my servants into sexual immorality and the eating of food sacrificed to idols."
(Revelation 2:20)

We hear of the city of Thyatira once in the book of Acts. It's the home of Lydia, a dealer in purple cloth, who hears Paul's message about Jesus and is baptized, along with the members of her family. She then invites Paul and his entourage to her home. This is the only time the Bible records any work done in the city of Thyatira, but we know from Revelation that there's a church there. We can easily see Lydia as being key in its formation.

Jesus speaks well of this church, affirming their deeds, their love, their faith, their service, and their perseverance. And he notes that they're doing more now than they once did. This confirms their spiritual growth. This is encouraging to see and provides a notable example for us to follow today.

Yet Jesus has one thing against them. They tolerate the false teaching of a self-proclaimed prophet, a woman named Jezebel. She misleads her followers to indulge in sexual immorality and eat food sacrificed to idols, which implies involvement in offering the sacrifices.

Does this duo of complaints—sexual immorality and eating idol-sacrificed meat—sound familiar? It's a repeated set of issues that we just saw at the church in Pergamum, who followed the false teachings of Balaam.

We, like these churches, must watch out for false teachers, specifically those who advocate ungodly sexual practices and worship that is contrary to what the Bible teaches.

Though Jesus has given Jezebel time to repent from her immoral teaching, she's refused to accept his offer and persists in leading people astray. The time for her punishment has come, along with all those who follow her. Unless they repent, they will suffer intensely along with her. In this way, all the churches will know of God's power and punishment for those who persist in misbehaving.

Only part of the church in Thyatira, however, has fallen prey to Jezebel's ungodly leadership. The rest have rejected her wayward instruction and Satanic teaching. To them, Jesus simply urges them to hold on to what they have until he returns.

Have we accepted any ungodly sexual practices in our lives or the church we attend? Is our worship rightly focused on the one true God?

[Discover more about what the Bible says about sexual immorality in Mark 7:21–22, Acts 15:20, Jude 1:7, and Revelation 9:21.]

DAY 8: THE CHURCH IN SARDIS: A DEAD CHURCH

REVELATION 3:1–6

"I know your deeds; you have a reputation of being alive, but you are dead." (Revelation 3:1)

A s with the churches in Smyrna and Pergamum, Scripture provides no additional information about the church in Sardis other than what occurs in the book of Revelation. Whereas Jesus has affirmed positive traits in each of the prior four churches, his feedback to the church in Sardis is a stinging rebuke.

Just like the other churches, he knows their deeds, the things they do. Though they have a reputation of being alive, they are not. We can assume that a positive reputation was at one time deserved, but it's no longer true. In fact, they're on life support. The church in Sardis is all but dead.

As a dead church, there's little they can do for Jesus.

He urges them to wake up.

He tells them to strengthen what little good remains. If they don't, their death will become final. As far as he's concerned, their work is unfinished. They have more to do, but they can't complete it in their present state.

Jesus calls them to remember the earlier days of their gathering, to recall what they received and heard. He urges them to hold on to it, to wake up and repent.

I wonder what churches he would similarly rebuke today. I wonder which of his followers he would say that to.

After his call to wake up and repent, Jesus adds a warning. He says he will come to them like a thief in the night, at a time they do not know. Though he doesn't indicate what he'll do when he shows up, we can assume punishment awaits them if they don't correct their errors.

This warning applies to most of the people in the church in Sardis, but not all. A few, Jesus notes, have not soiled their clothes. They've kept themselves clean and have continued to walk with him as worthy followers. He promises that their names will be forever written in the book of life.

What is the reputation of the church we attend? Despite its reputation, what might Jesus say? What do we need to repent of?

[Discover more about Jesus's book of life in Philippians 4:3, Revelation 20:15, and Revelation 21:27. Read about a good reputation in Esther 9:4 and 1 Timothy 3:7.]

DAY 9: THE CHURCH IN PHILADELPHIA: WEAK BUT WORTHY

REVELATION 3:7–13

"I know that you have little strength, yet you have kept my word and have not denied my name." (Revelation 3:8)

The church in Philadelphia is another church that only appears in Revelation. In Jesus's letter to them, he offers encouragement for both the present and the future.

The closest thing he has to criticism comes across more as an observation. He knows that they have little strength. He doesn't condemn them for being weak or command them to become strong. He does, however, acknowledge that despite having little strength, they have kept his word and not denied his name.

PETER DEHAAN

What encouragement this is for those of us who feel weak, lacking the faith-filled strength we see in others and not having it in ourselves. Even from our weakness, we—like the church in Philadelphia— can still accomplish what matters most. We can hold true to God's word, obeying what he says and living a life that honors him. We can also affirm Jesus as our Savior and not deny him before others. That is, we can tell others about him.

These qualities stand as two foundational traits of what it means when we follow Jesus: to do what he says and tell others about him.

Since the church in Philadelphia has kept Jesus's commands with patient endurance, he promises to shelter them from the future world-wide test, the hour of trial that is to come. They have proven themselves already and will not need to do so again. God will protect them from that onslaught.

He also reminds them that he's coming soon and encourages them to hold on to what they have. This isn't, however, permission to coast. It's an instruction to press forward in what they're already doing and finish the race strong. He promises to make the victors into a pillar—a central support structure, an element of strength—in God's temple. (See 1 Peter 2:4–6.)

If we perceive ourselves as weak, what can we do to follow the example of the church in Philadelphia? If we perceive ourselves as strong, how should we act?

[Discover more about weakness in Ezekiel 34:16, Joel 3:10, and 2 Corinthians 12:10. Read about strength in Romans 15:1 and 1 Peter 4:11.]

BONUS CONTENT: SATAN AT WORK

"I know where you live—where Satan has his throne."
(Revelation 2:13)

Satan is a reoccurring character in the book of Revelation who afflicts four of the seven churches Jesus addresses: Smyrna, Pergamum, Thyatira, and Philadelphia.

Two passages mention the "synagogue of Satan," one talks about his "so-called deep secrets," and the fourth says that his throne is in their city. Clearly Satan has his claws in over half of the seven churches. Do we have any reason to suspect his tactics are any different today?

Yet we don't need to cower in fear of Satan and

his schemes. Remember that we are on the winning side. God, the Creator, is more powerful than Satan, the created. Though Satan has limited power for a time, God's power is greater. That power is ours today if we will only use it.

How do we view Satan? How do we react to his efforts to corrupt the world and the church along with it?

[Discover more about Satan's role in these churches in Revelation 2:9, 2:13, 2:24, and 3:9.]

DAY 10: THE CHURCH IN LAODICEA: LUKEWARM FOR JESUS
REVELATION 3:14–22

"So, because you are lukewarm—neither hot nor cold—I am about to spit you out of my mouth." (Revelation 3:16)

We don't know that Paul ever traveled to Laodicea during his missionary journeys, but he mentions their church in his letter to the church in Colossae. He also wrote a letter to the church in Laodicea. We know this because he told the Colossian church to pass on their letter to Laodicea and for them to read Laodicea's. But that epistle is lost to history, and we don't have it to read today.

This leaves Jesus's message to the church in

Laodicea as our primary biblical source of information about them.

In this letter he accuses them of being lukewarm Christians and therefore worthless.

To understand being lukewarm, consider temperature extremes. If they're hot, they're on fire for Jesus. They'll advance his kingdom and be of great benefit. Conversely, if they're cold, they're worthless for any kingdom purpose, but they are at least in a place where they can repent, making a U-turn back to Jesus and becoming hot for him.

The lukewarm church—lacking either of these extremes—accomplishes nothing of value but isn't ready to repent either.

Though this is one understanding of this verse, consider another one.

Consider taking a drink. If the beverage is cool, it refreshes us. If the beverage is hot, it soothes us. But a lukewarm drink meets neither of these goals, and we don't want it. If we're expecting something hot or cold, a lukewarm beverage disappoints us, and we may spit it out.

Consider Jesus taking a metaphorical drink from the church in Laodicea. He expects either soothing hot or refreshing cold. Instead, he gulps a lukewarm drink of blah. He spits it out in disgust. What a terrifying image, for Jesus to find no value in us or our church and to figuratively spit us out in abhorrence.

This lukewarm church thinks they're well-off and doesn't need a thing. But Jesus's assessment of them is far different. He sees them as wretched, pitiful, poor, blind, and naked.

Yet he has a solution. He tells them to seek him for refined gold to make them rich; pure white clothes to cover themselves; and medicine to put on their eyes so they can see again.

Though his criticism is harsh, and his correction is stern, he reminds them that his rebuke and discipline come from his deep love for them.

What are they to do? Repent.

"Repent" is a recurring word in the book of Revelation, seen here more than in any other book in the Bible. Often, it's the recommended prescription for these seven churches.

What was true then may be true now.

Are we lukewarm for Jesus? What about the church we attend? What do we need to repent of?

[Discover more about *repent* in Matthew 4:17, Mark 6:12, Luke 13:3, and Acts 2:38.]

BONUS CONTENT: SUMMARY OF THE SEVEN CHURCHES' LETTERS

"Whoever has ears, let them hear what the Spirit says to the churches." (Revelation 3:22)

The New Testament includes many letters written to various churches. Other messages are addressed to individuals or groups. Paul wrote the most, but John, Peter, James, and Jude wrote epistles too.

The book of Revelation also has seven church letters. Unlike all the other ones, these come directly from Jesus. Though they apply specifically to the seven churches they're addressed to, we can learn from their messages.

Here's a summary of what Jesus commends them for and what he criticizes or warns them about:

Ephesus: They work hard, have patient endurance, don't tolerate evil, examine the claims of false apostles, and patiently suffer for Jesus (Revelation 2:2–3). They hate the evil deeds of the Nicolaitans, as Jesus does (Revelation 2:6).

But they don't love Jesus like they once did; they must repent (Revelation 2:4–5).

Smyrna: God knows what they're going through. They're spiritually rich, despite their sufferings and poverty. They endure slander (Revelation 2:9).

They have no reason to fear, even though they will suffer and face death, but they must remain faithful (Revelation 2:10).

Pergamum: They remain loyal to Jesus and refuse to deny him in the face of persecution (Revelation 2:13).

However, they've tolerated false teaching (Revelation 2:14). They must repent.

Thyatira: Jesus affirms their growing love, faith, service, and patient endurance (Revelation 2:19).

However, they've allowed a false prophet to lead them astray. They commit sexual sin and eat idol-offered food (Revelation 2:20); they must repent.

Sardis: Despite their reputation for being alive, they're dead. Their actions don't meet God's requirements (Revelation 3:1–2).

Yet some in the church have remained pure; they're worthy (Revelation 3:4).

Philadelphia: They obey God's word and haven't denied him, but they have little strength (Revelation 3:8). God will come to their aid.

Laodicea: They're lukewarm in their faith. They're arrogant, wretched, miserable, poor, blind, and naked (Revelation 3:15–17). Jesus has no reason to affirm them.

What can we personally emulate from these churches' good points? What might we need to reform in our practices today?

[Discover more about hearing what Jesus says in Matthew 13:15–16 and Mark 4:23.]

DAY 11: PRAISING GOD AS HOLY
REVELATION 4:1–8

"Holy, holy, holy is the Lord God Almighty." (Revelation 4:8)

Having considered Jesus's seven letters to the seven churches, we move forward into the third and longest part of the book of Revelation. Jesus, with a voice booming like a trumpet, explains what's about to occur. "Come," he roars to John. "I'll show you what must happen next." These events unfold in the remaining chapters of the book of Revelation.

In an instant John's spirit is whisked into heaven before a mighty throne. Father God sits on it. John describes what he sees, but it's challenging for us to grasp the imagery. Instead, we should merely stand in awe.

Circling God and his place of authority sit twenty-four more thrones. We can infer that these thrones are smaller and less important than God's. In each one of these twenty-four chairs sits an elder.

John describes the twenty-four elders as dressed in white and wearing gold crowns. From the Almighty's throne shoot bolts of lightning and resounding booms of thunder. In front of him blaze seven lamps, representing the sevenfold Spirit of God.

Enthroned in the center sits the Almighty God. Before him burn the lamps of the seven spirits. Surrounding them are the twenty-four elders. Between God's throne and the twenty-four elders are four living creatures.

Though John describes what these surreal beings look like, his words fall short of giving us an image we can fully comprehend. They have animal features, eyes cover their body, and they have six wings. Recall that seraphim also have six wings (Isaiah 6:2), but it's hard to imagine them looking like these four living creatures with their nonhuman traits and eyes everywhere.

Regardless of the appearance of the four living

creatures, it's what they do that matters. They spend all their time—day and night—praising God.

"Holy, holy, holy is the Lord God Almighty, who was, and is, and is to come" (Revelation 4:8).

The threefold repetition of *holy* is for emphasis. It's like adding a couple of exclamation points after the word holy or moving from holy, to more holy (two times), to most holy (three times). Father God, the Lord Almighty, is indeed most holy.

The four living creatures never stop chanting this.

If this worship of God sounds familiar, let's jump back to the book of Isaiah in the Old Testament, where the prophet recounts another instance where God is praised as "holy, holy, holy," this time by seraphim (Isaiah 6:2–3).

If the seraphim were praising God in Isaiah's time, and the four living creatures are doing it centuries later, might God have been receiving continuous praise between these two events? Might it still be happening today?

May we never forget that God exists as the highest form of holiness, worthy of our praise and adoration.

Do we praise God as "holy, holy, holy"? What can we do to worship God more fully?

[Discover more about the four living creatures in Revelation chapters 4–7 and Revelation 14:3, 15:7, 19:4, as well as Ezekiel 1:5–6. Read the parallel account in Isaiah 6:1–4.]

BONUS CONTENT: ETERNAL GOD

"The Lord God Almighty, who was, and is, and is to come."
(Revelation 4:8)

A recurring phrase in Revelation affirms the God who was, is, and is to come. This confirms that the Almighty existed in the past, is here in the present, and will be there in the future. He is eternal, without beginning or end.

God's eternal existence is hard for us to grasp from our time-bound perspective, but just because we have trouble understanding it doesn't mean it isn't real.

He was there at the beginning of time when he

created our world and us. He is with us now as we journey through life with him. And he will be there in the future, at the end of time, when he ushers in a new heaven and a new earth for the rest of eternity.

How can God's eternal nature inform our faith today? Do we believe that we will live with him in heaven for the rest of eternity?

[Discover more about eternal life in John 3:16–17, Romans 6:22–23, and Jude 1:21. See two verses similar to Revelation 4:8 in Revelation 1:4 and 1:8.]

DAY 12: PRAISING GOD AS WORTHY

REVELATION 4:9–11

"You are worthy, our Lord and God, to receive glory and honor and power." (Revelation 4:11)

The four living creatures have affirmed God as holy, holy, holy. The twenty-four elders are there too. What are they doing as the four living creatures chant their praise? Let's first consider the role of an elder.

When I think of an elder, I picture someone in a leadership position directing the activities of others and offering sage advice. In my mind, an elder is wiser than all others. We respect these elders with God-honoring awe for the position the Almighty has placed them in.

Yet we never see the twenty-four elders in Revelation leading others or offering wise advice. They seem to have but one function, one purpose. They worship Father God and his Son, Jesus, our Savior.

Each time the four living creatures call out their praise to the Father, the twenty-four elders respond by dropping from their thrones to bow down to the eternal God in reverent worship. This cycle repeats: the four living creatures praise God with their words and the twenty-four elders follow them by praising God with their actions.

At some point, however, the twenty-four elders dare to approach the throne of God. They've already fallen prostrate before him, so it's unlikely they'll stand to walk toward him. Instead, we can imagine them crawling in their reverent approach to the Almighty. Upon arriving at God's feet, they take off their gold crowns and lay them before their Lord.

Having given him their most exquisite gifts, they now add their verbal praise: "You are worthy, God, to receive glory, honor, and power. This is because you created everything through the strength of your will."

The twenty-four elders, along with the four

living creatures, worship God with their words of praise. In addition, the twenty-four elders worship God through their actions as they bow before him in admiration. They conclude their worship by giving him their gold crowns, representing their position of authority and power.

They give him their most valued possessions. And God deserves it.

Do we view God as worthy? What can we do through our words, actions, and gifts to let him know how we feel?

[Discover more about the twenty-four elders in Revelation 4:10, 5:8, 11:16, and 19:4.]

DAY 13: WHO ELSE IS WORTHY?
REVELATION 5

"You are worthy to take the scroll and to open its seals, because you were slain." (Revelation 5:9)

Our scene in heaven continues to unfold: the four living creatures have declared God holy, and the twenty-four elders have laid their crowns at the feet of Father God and proclaimed him worthy.

God, sitting on the throne, holds in his hand a scroll with seven seals that keep its contents secret. The scroll holds a message, but the seals prevent anyone from reading it. We anticipate hearing the message, but until someone opens it, we'll never know. We wait in expectation.

"Who," bellows an angel, "is qualified to open the scroll and show us what's inside?"

No one is. No one in heaven is worthy and no one on earth is worthy either. There is no one qualified to open the scroll and look inside.

This so distresses John that he weeps in disappointment. Until someone who is worthy comes forward, John can only wonder what the scroll says.

But an elder goes to comfort John, telling him not to cry. Someone is worthy and the elder knows who. It's the Lion of the tribe of Judah, the Root of David. These metaphorical labels allude to Jesus, a powerful Lion (ruler), a descendent of David from the tribe of Judah.

When John looks where the elder points, rather than a mighty lion he sees a weak lamb. It's the Lamb of God, sacrificed for us. Because of who he is and what he did, he is indeed worthy to open the scroll.

Jesus goes to God's throne and takes the document from his Father, preparing to break each of the seven seals so that he may open the scroll.

Then the four living creatures and the twenty-four elders fall before Jesus, the Lamb. Each one has a harp and golden bowls of incense, symbolizing the prayers of God's people.

Then they sing a new song.

"Jesus, you are worthy. You alone can open God's scroll because you died to save everyone, from everywhere. In doing so, you made them a kingdom of priests to serve God."

Jesus is worthy because he died for us. His sacrificial death qualifies him to open the scroll.

Do we believe that Jesus's death qualifies him to save us? Do we praise him as worthy?

[Discover more about being worthy in 2 Samuel 22:4, Matthew 10:37–38, Luke 7:6–8, and Hebrews 3:3.]

BONUS CONTENT: THE NUMBER SEVEN

The Lamb had seven horns and seven eyes, which are the seven spirits of God sent out into all the earth. (Revelation 5:6)

The number seven appears sixty-five times in the book of Revelation, showing up in thirty-six verses. Here's an overview of the key occurrences.

There are:

- Seven churches (first appearing in Revelation 1:4)
- Seven spirits (Revelation 1:4)
- Seven lampstands (Revelation 1:12)

- Seven stars (Revelation 1:20)
- Seven lamps (Revelation 4:5)
- Seven seals (Revelation 5:1)
- Seven horns (Revelation 5:6)
- Seven eyes (Revelation 5:6)
- Seven angels (Revelation 8:2)
- Seven trumpets (Revelation 8:6)
- Seven thunders (Revelation 10:4)
- Seven heads (Revelation 12:3)
- Seven crowns (Revelation 12:3)
- Seven plagues (Revelation 15:1)
- Seven bowls (Revelation 16:1)
- Seven hills (Revelation 17:9)
- Seven kings (Revelation 17:10)

God created us and our world in six days. He pronounced it as "very good" (Genesis 1:31). On the seventh day, he rested (Genesis 2:2). With this as our first encounter of the number seven in the Bible, we see it symbolizing completion, a fullness, even God's perfection.

As we continue reading the Bible, we come across the number seven over five hundred more times, with thirty-six showing up in Revelation alone.

Do we view the number seven as alluding to the perfection of God's creation? What is the significance of the number seven recurring throughout Revelation?

[Discover more about the number seven in Genesis 2:2, Ruth 4:15, Matthew 15:34–37, Mark 12:20–23, Luke 17:4, and Acts 6:1–3.]

DAY 14: BREAKING THE SEVEN SEALS
REVELATION 6

I watched as the Lamb opened the first of the seven seals.
(Revelation 6:1)

J esus has just been declared worthy to open God's scroll, that is, to access the words on the sealed document. One by one, Jesus will break each of the seven seals that hold the scroll closed. With each seal's removal, we'll get a hint at the contents inside, as if some of the scroll's prophecy escapes.

Jesus, the Lamb, breaks the first seal, and one of the four living creatures calls out, "Come!" A rider on a white horse gallops forth. He carries a bow, tasked with conquest.

As the Lamb breaks the second seal, the second living creature beckons, "Come!" A second rider sets out, this one on a fiery red horse. He has the power to take away peace from the whole earth so that people will kill each other.

When the Lamb breaks the third seal, the third living creature also cries out, "Come!" A third rider, mounted on a black horse, emerges. He holds a pair of scales, with the implied task of upsetting the economy and affecting the food supply.

With four remaining seals on the scroll, Jesus breaks another. The fourth living creature likewise calls, "Come!" A fourth horse, a pale steed, heads out ridden by Death. Hades follows close behind.

What has been revealed as Jesus breaks the first four seals doesn't sound like a message anyone would want to receive. And it's not for those who don't follow Jesus.

But for those who have remained true to their Savior, this is indeed a wonderful gift. At last judgment over evil is coming, and God will soon usher in a new heaven and a new earth. It's cause for them to celebrate. We get a hint of this as Jesus breaks open the next seal on the scroll.

With the opening of the fifth seal, John sees under the altar. There await the souls of the saints martyred for their faith. They call out to God, "How much longer until you judge the people of the earth?"

They're told to wait a little longer.

With the tearing of the sixth seal, a worldwide catastrophe unfolds, the beginning of an international apocalypse: the sun goes black, the moon turns red, and the stars fall from the sky. The heavens recede and the mountains and islands are removed.

The people who don't know God—from the greatest to the least—try to hide from him. They cower in fear. They call out for the rocks and mountains to fall on them and hide them from God's face and the wrath of Jesus.

John's vision lingers on this global catastrophe for a while in Revelation 7 before we see the breaking of the seventh and final seal in Revelation 8. It reveals the full contents and the power of the scroll's prophecy.

Will we hide from God's face or look forward to being in his presence? Do we fear Jesus's wrath or accept his gift of eternal life?

[Discover more about desperate people trying to hide from God in Hosea 10:8 and Luke 23:30.]

BONUS CONTENT: ZECHARIAH'S PROPHECY

There before me was a white horse! Its rider held a bow, and he was given a crown, and he rode out as a conqueror bent on conquest. (Revelation 6:2)

There are striking similarities between the Old Testament book of Zechariah and John's vision in Revelation. What God shows to John in the New Testament, he had already revealed much earlier in the Old Testament.

Consider this list of where some common Revelation phrases first showed up in the book of Zechariah.

- Red horse (Zechariah 1:8 and 6:2)
- White horse/horses (Zechariah 1:8 and 6:6)
- Black horse (Zechariah 6:2 and 6:6)
- Dappled/pale horse (Zechariah 6:6)
- Zion (Zechariah 1:14 and seven more verses)
- Four horns (Zechariah 1:18)
- Four winds (Zechariah 2:6)
- Seven eyes (Zechariah 3:9 and 4:10)
- Two olive trees (Zechariah 4:3 and 4:11)
- A gold/golden lampstand (Zechariah 4:2)
- Jerusalem (Zechariah 1:12 and thirty-nine other verses)
- A Holy Mountain (Zechariah 8:3)
- An earthquake (Zechariah 14:5)

Although there are more recurring words and themes linking the books of Zechariah and Revelation, these key phrases reveal a significant parallel between two time-distant prophecies and confirm God's singular plan for his creation.

*How can we better connect the Old and New Testaments?
How can we use Zechariah's prophecy to inform John's?*

[Read one of Zechariah's visions in Zechariah 1:7–21.]

DAY 15: THE MARK OF GOD
REVELATION 7:1–8

*"Do not harm the land or the sea or the trees until we put a
seal on the foreheads of the servants of our God."*
(Revelation 7:3)

Many people are familiar with the mark of the beast as revealed later in the book of Revelation, but what about the mark of God? What about the protection afforded to Jesus's followers who receive his seal on their foreheads?

But Bible teachers seldom mention the seal of God, while often addressing the mark of the beast. This unbalanced perspective produces unwarranted fear. Our focus should be on the seal of God and not the mark of the beast.

Hearing about the mark of the beast is indeed terrifying. It's something people must have if they're to buy or sell anything. Without having this sign on their right hand or forehead they'll be unable to do what they need to do to survive. However, those who don't comply—because of their refusal to worship the beast and receive his mark—could face martyrdom for their faith and beheading for telling others about Jesus.

Anyone who worships the beast and receives his mark will face God's fury and endure everlasting torment day and night. Those people will later break out in ugly, festering sores.

In his discussion of receiving the mark of the beast, John also mentions worshiping him. By receiving the mark of the beast, people implicitly worship him rather than Jesus. It's a disconcerting situation, giving us good reason to fear the end times and the mark of the beast.

Yet this misses the alternate symbol, having the seal of God on our foreheads. Though bearing God's mark will not save us from the beast's persecution, it will protect our lives and keep the beast from killing us.

Revelation says that some from the tribes of Israel will receive this seal of God and implies that many non-Jewish people will also receive it. They'll come from every nation, tribe, people, and language. This can include us.

As followers of Jesus, we can receive God's seal of protection and not fear the mark of the beast.

Do we fear the mark of the beast more than we relish the seal of God? How can we maintain our worship of God when faced with pressure to worship something else?

[Discover more about God putting his mark of protection on people in Genesis 4:15. Read more about the seal of God in Revelation 9:4–5.]

DAY 16: EVERYONE
REVELATION 7:9–12

Before me was a great multitude that no one could count, from every nation, tribe, people and language, standing before the throne and before the Lamb. (Revelation 7:9)

Immediately after John details how many people from the tribes of Israel receive the seal of God, he describes a great multitude, a throng too large to count. Given the context, we can assume they've also received God's seal on their foreheads.

This throng includes people who hail from every nation around the world. They represent every tribe, each race, and all languages. It's comforting to know that salvation through Jesus is available to everyone.

These people stand before the throne of God and Jesus. Dressed in white robes—signifying their pure standing through Jesus—they hold palm branches in their hands and wave them in a physical display of worship before their Lord.

Then they praise God with their voices, crying out that salvation belongs to Father God who sits on the throne and to the Lamb, Jesus his Son.

With this testimony given, the angels around the throne, along with the twenty-four elders and the four living creatures, affirm the words of these people. They fall prostrate and worship God, confirming the people's witness with a hearty "Amen!"

They give God praise, glory, wisdom, thanks, honor, power, and strength forever and ever. Then they confirm their worship with another "Amen!"

This glimpse of heavenly adoration can serve to inspire us to worship our Lord more fully today, with awestruck wonder.

Let's imagine ourselves in this supernatural setting. We stand before Father God and Jesus, his only Son. Clad in pure white robes we wave our palm branches in rhythmic adoration as we worship our Creator and Savior.

Then a multitude of angels, the twenty-four elders, and the four living creatures join us to confirm our praise. They fall before the Almighty in reverent worship.

What a glorious future awaits those of us who follow Jesus and remain true to him.

How can we use this imagery to better inform our worship of God today? How can we better ascribe to God praise, glory, wisdom, thanks, honor, power, and strength?

[Discover more about worshiping God for his salvation in Revelation 12:10 and 19:1. Read about worshiping Jesus with palm branches in John 12:13.]

DAY 17: SURVIVORS OF THE GREAT TRIBULATION
REVELATION 7:13–17

"These are they who have come out of the great tribulation;
they have washed their robes and made them white in the
blood of the Lamb." (Revelation 7:14)

I f you ask people to name the main phrases or themes from the book of Revelation, many would say the mark of the beast, the great tribulation, the millennium, and Armageddon. We've already discussed the mark of the beast. The millennium doesn't even appear in Revelation (though "a thousand years" shows up in Revelation 20) and Armageddon is only mentioned once (Revelation 16:16).

For all the discussion and speculation it generates, the word *tribulation* only occurs once in the entire Bible. And it's in this passage from Revelation. Given one scant mention of the *great tribulation*, it's perplexing to see all the conjecture this one idea has produced.

We'll make no attempt here to put to rest the many conflicting theories about what the great tribulation means and when it will take place. Remember, Jesus says no one knows when this will happen, except for the Father. So why attempt to uncover what Jesus says we can't know?

What we do know about the great tribulation comes from this one verse. We can confirm, quite simply, that it will happen, and that some people will survive it. That's it. That's all the Bible teaches about the great tribulation.

These survivors of the great tribulation will have their robes washed white, purified by Jesus's saving death, which he offered as a once-and-for-all sacrifice to make us right with Father God.

In John's vision, one of the elders explains the outcome awaiting those who survive the great tribulation. *This* should be our focus, not the unknowable understanding of *when*.

The survivors of the great tribulation will serve God around the clock in his temple and before his throne. He will shelter them with his presence.

They are in a safe place at last. The pain and agony of life will no longer assault them. They will never again be hungry or thirsty, with the need for physical sustenance no longer an issue. And the sun won't afflict their labors with scorching heat anymore.

Jesus will be their shepherd. He will give them springs of living water to drink. And Father God will dry their tears.

What do we most anticipate about spending eternity in heaven with God? Have we received Jesus's living water?

[Discover more about Jesus's living water in John 4:13–14 and 7:38. Read about living water in the Old Testament in Jeremiah 2:13, Jeremiah 17:13, and Zechariah 14:8.]

DAY 18: SILENCE FROM THE SEVENTH SEAL

REVELATION 8:1–5

When he opened the seventh seal, there was silence in heaven for about half an hour. (Revelation 8:1)

Finally, Jesus breaks the seventh and final seal of Father God's scroll. At the opening of each of the first six seals, something immediately happened in John's vision. Usually this related to judgment for the wicked or justice for the persecuted. What happens with the opening of the seventh seal?

Nothing. Absolutely nothing.

Nothing, that is, if we count silence as nothing. But silence before a holy and awe-inspiring God is much more than nothing. It's a profound form of worship. In fact, it could be the most meaningful display of adoration we can offer.

And with the scroll finally opened before everyone to reveal all, their only response is silence. All of heaven quiets for half an hour in reverent astonishment over the contents of the scroll and the God behind it.

Remember the seven living creatures and the twenty-four elders praising God in song? Recall the angels joining in? And remember the white-robed saints crying out to God in praise?

Silence.

They all go silent for thirty minutes. This doesn't mean they stop worshiping God. It means they shift their worship from audible praise to silent adoration. It's what God deserves. It's the right response to his intent to judge those who don't follow him and his plan to usher in a new heaven and a new earth.

There are times—many times perhaps—where the proper response to God is not words or action, but silence. Yet many today squirm at even a few seconds of quiet. A minute of silence is beyond their ability to endure. And a half-hour exceeds their comprehension.

Yet the psalmist records the Almighty telling us

to "Be still, and know that I am God" (Psalm 46:10). How often do we do this? Have we ever done it?

Take a moment now to be silent before God, removing all audible distractions and verbal responses. Still your racing mind and quiet your pounding heart before our Creator and Savior. In this way, you will worship him in a most profound way, without sound or movement.

May he receive our quiet as our highest form of worship.

Do we see silence as a proper way to praise God? How can we master the art of being still before Almighty God?

[Discover more about the instruction to *be still* in Exodus 14:14, Nehemiah 8:11, Psalm 37:7, and Zechariah 2:13.]

DAY 19: SEVEN TRUMPETS AND THREE WOES
REVELATION 8:6–13

I heard an eagle that was flying in midair call out in a loud voice: "Woe! Woe! Woe to the inhabitants of the earth, because of the trumpet blasts about to be sounded by the other three angels!" (Revelation 8:13)

With the seventh seal broken and the contents of the scroll revealed, God gives seven angels seven trumpets. These seven angels may be the same ones we saw in Revelation 1:20, represented by the seven stars, the seven angels of the seven churches. Or they may be a different group. This detail doesn't matter as much as what the angels do with their trumpets and what happens as each one of them plays.

They bring their trumpets to their mouths in preparation to sound them.

The first angel blows his trumpet. Hail and fire afflict the earth. One third of the world, one third of the trees, and all the grass burns up.

The second angel sounds his trumpet. A large mountain-like mass hurls into the sea, turning one third of it to blood. One third of the sea creatures die and one third of the ships sink.

The third angel plays his trumpet. A great star —an asteroid perhaps—blazes through the sky like a torch and falls to earth. One third of the rivers turn bitter and many people die when they drink its water.

The fourth angel blows his trumpet. The lights in the sky dim. One third of the sun, one third of the moon, and one third of the stars go dark. There is no light for one third of the day and one third of the night.

Before the fifth trumpet sounds, however, an eagle soars overhead. He calls out a warning of woe to the rest of the earth for what the final three trumpets will usher in.

But what is "woe"? It's not a word we often hear today.

Woe is a noun. Though it can mean regret, in

this case it means misfortune or a cause for misery. Three woes await the inhabitants of earth, one ushered in with each of the three remaining trumpet blasts, which we can expect will produce even more havoc than the first four.

This is what awaits those who don't follow Jesus.

Does the end-time imagery in the book of Revelation cause us to fear? What woes do we have now and how should we respond to them?

[Discover more about woe in Psalm 120:5, Matthew 23:13–36, Luke 6:24–26, and Jude 1:11.]

DAY 20: SOME STILL WILL NOT REPENT

REVELATION 9

The rest of mankind who were not killed by these plagues still did not repent of the work of their hands. (Revelation 9:20)

After the opening of the scroll's seventh and final seal, seven angels receive seven trumpets. The first four have already blown their instruments, which resulted in affliction for much of the earth. Three trumpets remain, accompanied by three woes.

The fifth angel sounds his trumpet. The star that fell to earth when the third angel blew his horn holds the key to the Abyss. He now unlocks and opens it. Smoke, as if from a giant furnace, bellows forth, darkening the sun and sky. Locusts emerge from the smoke.

These insects have scorpion-like power. But God only allows them to afflict those who do not have his seal on their foreheads; those with his mark are safe.

The locusts torture, but cannot kill, the people who lack God's seal. The agony of these people is so great that they long to die, but they cannot. The locusts go out as an army—led by their king, called Destroyer—to torment the people for five months.

What an agonizing time for those who don't carry God's seal upon them.

This is the first woe. Two more are to come.

The sixth angel blows his trumpet. A voice comes from the four horns of God's altar. It tells the angel to release four other angels waiting for this day at the Euphrates River. These angels have been kept at the ready for this final hour and now go out to kill one third of all the people. They lead a formidable cavalry of two hundred million soldiers. A terrifying killing machine, they wipe out one third of the people.

This is the second woe.

Given all that's happened to the remaining people, we'd think that they'd receive all this affliction as a warning from God to turn from their evil ways and repent. They don't.

They persist in doing what they've always done: the actions God views as sin and of missing his mark. They continue their worship of demons and other hand-made idols that can't see, hear, or walk. They do not repent of committing murder, of using magic arts, of sexual immorality, or of theft.

There's still more to come before we get to the seventh angel and his trumpet in Revelation 11.

What do we need to repent of? Though we don't yet live in this end-time situation, which behaviors should we change today?

[Discover more about the need to repent, which occurs more in John's vision than in any other book in the Bible, in Revelation 2:5, 2:16, 2:21–22, 3:3, 3:19, 9:20–21, and 16:9–11.]

DAY 21: THE END IS NEAR
REVELATION 10

"There will be no more delay!" (Revelation 10:6)

John's vision takes a bit of a diversion before the seventh and final trumpet. After the sixth trumpet blast, we'd expect people to repent of their wrongdoing. They don't. They persist in their sinful behavior.

At this point, another angel descends from heaven. Robed in a cloud, with a rainbow above him, his face looks like the sun and his legs resemble pillars of fire. He plants one leg on land and the other on the sea. He holds another scroll, a small one. This one isn't sealed.

With his right hand raised toward heaven, he

declares, "There will be no more delay!" That is, the end is near. To make sure we realize he's not saying these words of his own accord, he avows he's stating the truth in the name of eternal God, the God of creation. This angel is the mouthpiece of the Almighty.

At last, judgment on the unrepentant is about to occur. From Genesis 3 (after Adam and Eve sinned), the rest of Scripture has been moving steadily toward this conclusion: a new heaven and a new earth to replace what we know now. All who follow Jesus will live with him there for the rest of eternity. This has been God's plan since the beginning.

With the end about to take place, we can utter a sigh of relief. At last, eternity approaches. While we look forward to the pristine paradise that awaits us —one reminiscent of God's first created paradise in Eden—let's not lose sight of making the most of our life while we're still on this earth. God has a plan for each of us to fulfill in our remaining time here. May we do what he has called us to do and finish strong before we join him in his everlasting paradise.

The seventh trumpet blast and the third woe are all that remain before God's finale unfolds. "This," the angel says, "will accomplish the mystery of God."

John goes to the angel with the tiny scroll and asks for it. The angel tells John to eat it. John does, and it melts in his mouth like sweet-tasting honey, but it turns sour in his gut. Then he's told to continue prophesying.

It's an implication that what John has to say may not sit well with his audience.

How can we make the most of our remaining time here on earth as we look forward to our future in heaven? How should we react if people don't like what God tells us to say?

[Discover what Paul says about God's mystery in Romans 11:25–27, Romans 16:25–27, 1 Corinthians 2:7, Ephesians 3:2–9, Colossians 1:25–27, and 1 Timothy 3:16.]

DAY 22: TWO WITNESSES
REVELATION 11:1–14

"And I will appoint my two witnesses, and they will prophesy for 1,260 days." (Revelation 11:3)

As we work our way through the second of three woes, we come across two witnesses. God appoints them to prophesy for 1,260 days, almost three and a half years. In a bit of intriguing imagery, God refers to them as two olive trees and two lampstands.

Centuries earlier, the prophet Zechariah mentioned two olive trees in his future-focused prophecy in Zechariah 4. He says God anoints these two olive trees to serve him. Zechariah also sees these two olive trees standing on either side of a golden lampstand, which holds seven lamps.

Looking just at the book of Revelation, we see seven lampstands in Chapter 1 referring to the seven churches. But here the two lampstands refer to two people. These two witnesses have extraordinary power. If anyone tries to hurt them, flames will shoot from their mouths to kill their attackers.

They also have power over the weather and can cause a drought to occur (consider 1 Kings 17:1). They can turn water into blood (consider Exodus 7:14–20). They can also afflict the earth with plagues whenever they want to.

God protects them and gives them great power. Yet when they finish all that he calls them to do— their 1,260 days of testifying about him—the beast attacks them and kills them, martyring them for their obedient witness for God.

That's not the outcome we'd expect for such powerful people who do exactly what God tells them to do. Yet they die anyway.

The people on earth refuse to bury these two witnesses. Instead, they celebrate their death by giving presents to each other. They're happy because these two prophets had tormented everyone on earth. We don't know if this is because of their words or their actions, but we do know the people didn't receive it well. This shouldn't surprise us. Jesus said that as his followers and disciples everyone will hate us.

But God doesn't forget the two witnesses. After three and a half days, the Almighty breathes life into their lifeless bodies. They resurrect and stand. Fear grips everyone. God calls them home, whisking them up to heaven in a cloud (consider 2 Kings 2:11).

The earth quakes, destroying one tenth of the city. Thousands die, and the survivors give glory to God.

This ends the second woe. The third is about to begin.

How should we respond if the world hates us? (And what does it say about us if they don't?) How willing are we to be God's witnesses, regardless of the cost?

[Discover more about the hate unbelievers will have toward Jesus's followers in Matthew 10:22, Matthew 24:9, Mark 13:13, Luke 21:17, and John 15:18–19.]

BONUS CONTENT: THE THIRD WOE

The second woe has passed; the third woe is coming soon.
(Revelation 11:14)

John writes that the third woe is coming, but he never directly says what this third woe is. Bible scholars disagree on what it refers to and, aside from speculation, we can't really know.

Here are five considerations:

1. The third woe occurs in the passage following this verse, which happens right after the seventh trumpet sounds (Revelation 11:15–19). Yet this passage

doesn't sound like an account of woe but one of triumph.

2. Another thought is that the third woe occurs the next time the word appears in Revelation. This would make it Revelation 12:12. Heavens rejoice but woe to the earth.

3. Another possibility is that the third woe occurs in Revelation 18:9–24, with the word woe appearing six times in the text, each time in couplets, which emphasizes just how bad the woe is. The passage warns of judgment.

4. The next consideration is that the third woe includes everything that happens after Revelation 11:14, ending at Revelation 19:21.

5. A final thought also starts the third woe at Revelation 11:14, with an alternate ending point for the third woe at Revelation 20:15, which marks the transition to a new heaven and a new earth.

Which is it?
We don't know. God does.

We must be content to hold this question loosely and embrace the mystery of it without needing to know a definitive answer. Remember, whether we rightly resolve the specifics about the third woe or not, whatever happens will happen.

The point is that the third woe is bad, and we don't want to experience it.

How content are we to not know the precise meaning of the third woe? We can spend a lifetime trying to understand Scripture, but some things will always remain a mystery. Are we okay with that?

[Discover more about understanding God in Mark 4:33, Luke 24:45, 1 Corinthians 2:12, Philemon 1:6, and 1 John 5:20.]

DAY 23: WORSHIP
REVELATION 11:15–19

And the twenty-four elders, who were seated on their thrones
before God, fell on their faces and worshiped God.
(Revelation 11:16)

With the second woe complete, the seventh angel sounds his trumpet. Whereas the first six trumpet blasts bring forth immediate death and destruction to the earth, the seventh and final one does not—at least not at first.

Instead, it unleashes words.

Loud voices from heaven proclaim Jesus as the new ruler over the kingdom of the world. He will reign over it forever, for the rest of eternity.

And how do the twenty-four elders respond?

They fall from their thrones and prostrate themselves to worship God. Not only is their worship a physical display of reverence, but they also praise him with their voices. It doesn't matter if they sing this, chant this, or recite it in unison. The key point is that they give words of adoration to God as an offering of sincere worship.

They open by thanking God as the Lord God Almighty, affirming him for his presence now and his work in the past. He has used his great power, they say, and begun to reign on earth, but the people were angry and God's wrath against them has come.

He will judge the dead and reward his servants and those who revere him. He will destroy those who destroyed his creation.

As the twenty-four elders complete their tribute to God, his temple in heaven opens to reveal the ark of his covenant inside. Lightning flashes, rumbles occur, thunder peals, the earth quakes, and hail pelts the earth. What an incredible response to the twenty-four elders' adoration.

The twenty-four elders encircle God's throne, poised to reverence him. As revealed earlier in Revelation, worshiping the Almighty is their only job. This should give us a fresh perspective on what it means to worship our Creator and Savior.

For many, worship means singing a few songs on Sunday morning. Yet worship can—and should—occur throughout our week. We can worship God through our words and through our actions. Everything we do has the potential to worship our Lord—or disappoint him. We can worship God when we're at peace or distraught, regardless of the outcome. We can worship him in the Spirit and in truth (John 4:23–24). And we can offer ourselves as a living sacrifice (Romans 12:1).

With God now having appropriately received the praise and worship due him, we're poised for the third and final woe to unfold.

What do we do to worship God? What can we learn from the twenty-four elders so we can praise the Almighty more fully?

[Discover more about worship in Job 1:20, Psalm 100:2, John 4:23–24, and Romans 12:1.]

DAY 24: THE BLOOD OF THE LAMB
REVELATION 12

They triumphed over him by the blood of the Lamb and by the word of their testimony. (Revelation 12:11)

The phrase "the blood of the Lamb" only appears in the book of Revelation and then just twice. We referred to the first occurrence in "Day 17: Survivors of the Great Tribulation." This passage is the second mention. Here's what happens:

A woman is in labor. Near her stands a dragon who opposes her and her son. Yet God protects the woman and her newborn baby, thwarting the dragon's intention to kill her child.

A supernatural war breaks out in heaven with

Michael and his angel army fighting against the dragon and his angels. The outmatched dragon faces defeat and is hurled out of heaven, along with his minions. He can no longer appear before Father God to accuse us.

In this passage John gives us a key to better understand his vision. He clarifies that the dragon is the ancient serpent, implicitly the one who caused Adam and Eve to sin. This dragon is also known as the devil and Satan. This means that the dragon, the serpent, the devil, and Satan are various names for the same evil spiritual being that opposes Father God, Jesus, and us.

After the dragon's ouster from God's presence, a loud voice booms from heaven. It declares that salvation, the kingdom of God, and the authority of Jesus have now come in full at last. The enemy has been defeated.

This occurs because of the blood of the Lamb, that is, because of Jesus's sacrificial death.

The concept of the need for spilt blood occurs throughout the Bible, in both the Old and New Testaments. We get the first allusion to the shedding of blood when Abel offers an animal sacrifice to God (Genesis 4:2-4).

The concept fully develops when God decrees

the need for yearly animal sacrifices to make the people right with him (Leviticus 16:34 and Hebrews 10:3–5). This is to cover their mistakes (their sins), with an animal dying in their place. In doing so, God atones for their shortcomings; he redeems them.

This need for ongoing sacrificial deaths occurs throughout the Old Testament. But Jesus, the Lamb of God, comes to fulfill that requirement once and for all. He spills his blood when he dies to make us right with his Father in heaven and prepare us to live with him there forever. This is what the blood of the Lamb has done—and will do—for us.

Thank you, Jesus, for your sacrificial death that gives us eternal life.

What does the blood of the Lamb mean to you? What should be our response to Jesus dying in our place?

[Discover more about the blood of Jesus in Romans 5:9, Ephesians 1:7–8, Hebrews 9:11–28, 1 Peter 1:18–19, and 1 John 1:7.]

BONUS CONTENT: DANIEL AND REVELATION

Then war broke out in heaven. Michael and his angels fought against the dragon, and the dragon and his angels fought back. (Revelation 12:7)

I n reading Daniel's four prophecies in the book named after him, we see several phrases parallel to the book of Revelation. This suggests a consistency between Daniel's future-focused visions and John's.

Consider these similarities:

- Ten horns in Daniel 7:7, 7:20, and 7:24 and Revelation 12:3 and 13:1.

- Four horns in Daniel 8:8, 8:22, and Revelation 9:13. (Also in Ezekiel 43:20 and Zechariah 1:18.)
- The angel Michael in Daniel 10:13, Daniel 10:21 and Revelation 12:7. (The only other time the Bible mentions Michael is in Jude 1:9.)
- One coming with the clouds in Daniel 7:13 and Revelation 1:7.
- The books were opened in Daniel 7:10 and Revelation 20:12.
- A command to seal the scroll in Daniel 12:4 and to open the sealed scroll in Revelation 5:1–2, 5, 9. Might this be the same scroll? (Compare this to the command for John to *not* seal the scroll containing the prophecy in Revelation 22:10.)

How do we react to the similarity between the visions of Daniel and John? How can these connections between the Old and New Testaments fill us with awe?

[Read about Jesus coming on the clouds in Matthew 24:30, Matthew 26:64, and Mark 14:62.]

DAY 25: WHOEVER HAS EARS
REVELATION 13

Whoever has ears, let them hear. (Revelation 13:9)

After the expulsion of the dragon (that is, Satan, the devil) from heaven, he comes to earth and waits at the seashore. A beast emerges and the dragon gives him power. The beast blasphemes God, slandering God's name, heaven, and the people who live there.

He fights against the Lord's people on earth and wins. He receives authority over all who remain and everyone whose name does *not* appear in the Lamb's book of life now worships the beast.

At this point, John writes, "Whoever has ears, let them hear."

If this phrase sounds familiar, it's because we've already seen it seven times in the book of Revelation. This phrase wraps up each of the letters to the seven churches. In each case, Jesus shares with them his message of encouragement and correction and then says, "Whoever has ears, let them hear what the Spirit says to the churches."

Reading his letters is not enough. They must hear them too. So must we.

In this passage, the phrase occurs an eighth time, encouraging us to take to heart John's message, to really hear what he says. And what are we supposed to hear? The words that precede it.

In this case it's a warning that everyone whose name does *not* appear in Jesus's book of life will worship the beast. This implies that those of us whose names *are* in the Lamb's book of life will not succumb to this false worship.

Our right standing with Jesus will keep us focused on him and not the beast. We will prevail through our Savior.

The message is simple: we want our names in the book of life. We do this when we follow Jesus and become his disciple.

There are many times, however, when the Bible talks about people who have ears but cannot hear.

God's message is there for them, but they can't comprehend it. That's why it's important for us to hear what God is saying and respond before it's too late and we risk losing the ability to understand it.

Say yes to Jesus today.

Do we have ears that hear what Jesus is saying? How should we react to his message?

[Discover more about ears that hear in 1 Chronicles 17:20, Job 42:5, Proverbs 20:12, and Isaiah 32:3. Read where else Jesus says "Whoever has ears, let them hear" in Matthew 11:1–15, 13:1–9, and 13:36–43.]

DAY 26: THE HARVEST
REVELATION 14

"Take your sickle and reap, because the time to reap has come, for the harvest of the earth is ripe." (Revelation 14:15)

A heading later added to Revelation 14:6 in some Bibles says, "The Three Angels." Yet a careful reading of this chapter reveals seven.

The first angel flies in midair to warn the people of the coming judgment and urge them to give God glory and worship him (Revelation 14:6–7).

The second angel announces that Babylon has fallen (Revelation 14:8).

The third angel warns that anyone who

worships the beast and wears his mark will receive everlasting torment (Revelation 14:9–13).

A fourth angel, one "like a son of man," comes next. He wears a golden crown and carries a sickle (Revelation 14:14). Though this could be a veiled reference to Jesus—and some think it is—the rest of Revelation refers to Jesus more directly, so we can accept this as an angel who looks *like* Jesus, as one who *resembles* the Son of Man (Son of God).

The fifth angel comes out of the temple and encourages the fourth angel to begin harvesting, for the time has come and the harvest is ripe. The fourth angel does just that (Revelation 14:15–16).

A sixth angel comes from the temple, also carrying a sickle (Revelation 14:17).

Still another angel, the seventh one, who oversees the fire on the altar, encourages the sixth one to begin the grape harvest (Revelation 14:18). The angel does, throwing the grapes he picks into God's winepress of wrath. Blood flows.

The purpose of the seven angels in this evocative passage is to bring about the harvest over the whole earth.

When it's time to harvest their crops, farmers can't increase the yield. It's too late. The time to affect the outcome has already passed. This comes earlier in the season when the crop is planted, tilled, weeded, and watered.

This means that what we do *now* can increase God's harvest later.

How can we plant and water seeds for Jesus? What can we do to increase God's harvest?

[Discover more about planting and harvesting in Matthew 9:37–38, Matthew 13:1–30, Luke 10:1–3, and 1 Corinthians 3:6–8. Read two other verses that reference someone *like a son of man* in Daniel 7:13 and Revelation 1:13.]

DAY 27: SEVEN PLAGUES TO COMPLETE GOD'S WRATH
REVELATION 15

I saw in heaven another great and marvelous sign: seven angels with the seven last plagues—last, because with them God's wrath is completed. (Revelation 15:1)

Revelation 15 seems out of order. In it seven plagues of God's wrath are unleashed even though his harvest already took place in Revelation 14. Yet for our purpose in applying John's vision to us today, it doesn't matter if the order of these events is chronological or not.

Regardless, we're winding down God's judgment and moving ever closer to the glorious new heaven and new earth where we'll live with him for all of eternity.

In this chapter we meet seven angels. They may be the ones from Revelation 14, or they could be different. Regardless, they have seven plagues, the last of God's afflictions. These plagues will conclude God's wrath on a rebellious people who have repeatedly dismissed the Almighty, despite many opportunities to repent.

This emerges as an exciting time for those who have resisted worshiping the beast and did not give in to his demands. They sing their praises to God, proclaiming him as marvelous and glorious. He, and he alone, is truly holy.

In the temple in heaven, the tabernacle opens, and seven angels appear, carrying with them the seven plagues. One of the four living creatures gives each angel a bowl of wrath.

This wrath—the final wrath that God will inflict on the earth—does not suggest he's a mean deity, malevolently inflicting punishment on his creation. Instead, it's an act of love.

How can pestilence and wrath be an act of love?

They're God's final effort to get as many of the

remaining people on earth to repent, to make a U-turn from what they're doing to follow him. This will prepare them to join him in eternity.

They've already had chances to turn to him throughout their life, with several more opportunities occurring in Revelation. These seven plagues are God's last attempt to get their attention and draw them into his everlasting family.

God used plagues repeatedly in the Old Testament. The best known occur when he sent plagues to Egypt to convince Pharaoh to let his people go (Exodus 7–12). The afflictions were to get Pharaoh's attention. When God sends plagues at other times, however, it's to get *his people's* attention. Though extreme, sometimes it's the only thing that works.

John covers the effect of these final plagues— God's bowls of wrath—in Revelation 16, but for now our focus is on the Lord God Almighty. The temple fills with awe-inducing smoke that comes from God's glory and power. Until the angels can unleash these seven plagues on the rest of humanity, no one can enter the temple.

What has God had to do to get our attention? When he takes extreme action, do we draw closer to him or blame him for what we're suffering?

[Discover more about plagues in Leviticus 26:25, Numbers 11:33, Psalm 106:28–29, and Amos 4:10. Read more about God's wrath in Numbers 16:46, Ezekiel 6:12, Luke 21:23, and John 3:36.]

BONUS CONTENT: RECURRING REFERENCES

Out of the temple came the seven angels with the seven plagues. (Revelation 15:6)

W e encounter many recurring references in the book of Revelation. Here are three.

Seven Angels

These are only mentioned in Revelation. We begin with the seven angels to the seven churches starting in Revelation 1:20. Next we see seven angels standing before God with seven trumpets in Revelation 8:2. Then we count seven angels in

Revelation 14:6–19. Last, we have seven angels with seven plagues and seven bowls in Revelation 15 and following.

We don't know if these are four distinct groups of seven angels or the same seven angels who keep showing up. Regardless, they come from God and do his bidding.

1,260 days

This number occurs only in Revelation 11:3 and Revelation 12:6. It's approximately forty-two months, which also shows up in Revelation 13:5. Forty-two months is about three and a half years, which we might infer comes from the phrase *time, times and half a time*. This interesting notation occurs in Revelation 12:14, as well as Daniel 7:25 and Daniel 12:7.

Do these references to this 1,260-day time-frame all refer to the same span or to three or four different ones? If we read Revelation sequentially, we must embrace multiple three-and-a-half-year eras. Yet if they all refer to the same event, then Revelation chapters 11 through 13 are concurrent and not chrono-logical.

Ten Horns and Seven Heads

We see this characteristic of ten horns and seven heads given to a red dragon in Revelation 12:3. Later, Revelation 13:1 mentions a beast with ten horns and seven heads. Finally, is a woman riding a scarlet beast that bears blasphemous names and has seven heads and ten horns in Revelation 17:3.

Is this the same creature appearing at various times with different descriptions? Or is it three different creatures, each one with ten horns and seven heads? If so, the threefold repetition is significant.

Though the unanswered questions that arise from these recurring references in the book of Revelation may be unsettling, remember that God holds the answers and that should be enough for us.

Does not knowing the answers to these questions produce frustration or draw us to God in awe of his omniscient greatness? When we read something in the Bible we don't understand, do we skim by it or study it even more thoroughly?

[Discover the meaning of the ten horns and seven heads in Revelation 17:9–14.]

DAY 28: A THIEF IN THE NIGHT
REVELATION 16:1–16

"Look, I come like a thief! Blessed is the one who stays awake and remains clothed, so as not to go naked and be shamefully exposed." (Revelation 16:15)

A voice bellows out from the temple, commanding the seven angels to go forth and unleash their seven bowls of wrath.

The first angel pours out his bowl on the land, releasing disgusting, festering sores on everyone who bears the mark of the beast.

The second angel follows and pours out his bowl of wrath on the sea. The water turns to blood and every creature in the sea dies.

The third angel empties his bowl of God's wrath on the drinkable water. It, too, becomes blood. The angel explains that it's because they killed God's holy people and messengers. As a result of their bloodshed, they must now drink blood.

The fourth angel afflicts the sun. He intensifies its heat, scorching the people with fire. In searing pain, they curse God, refusing to repent and give him glory.

The fifth angel pours out his wrath on the beast's throne, plunging his kingdom into darkness. The people writhe in agony and curse God, but again, they refuse to repent.

The sixth angel pours out his bowl on the Euphrates River. Instead of turning it to blood, however, it dries up. No longer is the great river a physical barrier to keep armies away; their path to attack is now open. From the mouths of the dragon, the beast, and the false prophet spring demonic spirits that resemble frogs. They solicit kings from around the globe amass for a great battle.

Then Jesus warns that he'll come like a thief in the night, at a time when people don't expect him. Yet he will bless all who stay alert—awaiting his return—for their diligence.

This isn't the first time Jesus uses the imagery of

a thief. In his own end-time prophecy during his life here on earth, he warns us to keep watch because we don't know when he'll return. His coming will be like a thief coming under the cover of darkness when most people are asleep and unaware (Matthew 24:36–44 and Luke 12:35–40).

Jesus follows this up with a more accessible example in his parable of the ten virgins. They're waiting for the groom to arrive so the wedding celebration can begin. Some run out of oil for their lamps, while the others have prepared for a long wait and brought extra oil. Jesus ends this parable with the warning to keep watch because we don't know when he'll return (Matthew 25:1–13).

Are we looking for Jesus's return, staying alert and ready? Do we live our life as if Jesus could return at any moment?

[Discover more about a thief in the night in 1 Thessalonians 5:1–9 and 2 Peter 3:10.]

DAY 29: IT IS DONE
REVELATION 16:17–21

The seventh angel poured out his bowl into the air, and out of the temple came a loud voice from the throne, saying, "It is done!" (Revelation 16:17)

Jesus has just warned everyone to remain ready for his return, which will happen as unexpectedly as a thief coming under the cover of darkness.

Then the seventh angel arrives. He pours out his bowl into the air. Immediately, a voice thunders from the temple. The sound comes from the throne and says, "It is done!"

In response to this exciting proclamation, lightning flashes, the earth rumbles, and thunder peals.

A severe earthquake follows with unprecedented intensity. The great city—figuratively Sodom and Egypt (Revelation 11:8)—splits into three parts. Other cities throughout the nations collapse. Islands disappear and mountains level.

Hundred-pound hailstones fall from the sky. The people curse God because of this terrible plague, yet the Bible doesn't mention any of them turning to him.

Since the voice proclaiming, "It is done!" comes from God's throne in the temple, we can assume that these are the words of the Lord God Almighty.

With his final plague, the last bowl of wrath, unleashed to get the people's attention, there will be no more. It is done, at last.

The results of this final plague reach completion, opening the door for the concluding events that must occur before God can unveil a new heaven and a new earth for his people.

Father God says, "It is done!"

Earlier, Jesus says a similar phrase. As he's dying on the cross to save all humanity throughout all history, his final words before he breathes his last are, "It is finished." Then he bows his head and dies (John 19:30).

Jesus's death, of course, isn't the end. Instead,

it's the first step toward a new beginning. He is buried, but three days later he rises from the dead. In doing so he proves he has mastery over death. When we follow him—as he repeatedly invites us to do—we, too, will enjoy eternal life through him and with him.

When Jesus says, "It is finished," he ushers in a new way for us to receive his salvation, a solution far superior to the Old Testament rules and regulations.

When Father God says, "It is done," he accomplishes what must occur so that he can usher in a new heaven and a new earth. It's there we'll spend eternity with him and Jesus.

Are we following Jesus? Do we look forward to eternity in God's new heaven and new earth?

[Discover more about following Jesus in Matthew 4:19, Mark 2:14, Luke 9:23, and John 12:26.]

DAY 30: THE LAMB WILL OVERCOME
REVELATION 17

"They will wage war against the Lamb, but the Lamb will triumph over them because he is Lord of lords and King of kings—and with him will be his called, chosen and faithful followers." (Revelation 17:14)

With God's final wrath complete, we can now move steadily toward his plan for a new heaven and a new earth. Only a few remaining events must happen before we get there.

The first relates to the great prostitute.

The seventh angel, the one who poured out the final bowl of wrath, comes to John and says he will show him what punishment awaits the great prostitute. We've not met her before in Revelation, so she appears as a new player. Calling her "great," however, may mislead our understanding of her and what she represents. "Nefarious" may be a better label.

The angel takes John into the desert.

There he sees a woman, sitting on a beast, dressed in purple and scarlet, glittering with gold, precious gems, and pearls. She holds a cup filled with abominations and the filth of her adulteries. Written on her forehead we see her title, which tells us that she is the mother of prostitutes and all abominations.

She is Babylon the Great.

Since the Bible has already recorded the fall of Babylon (Daniel 5:30–31), we know that this is not a reference to the historical Babylonian Empire, but a characterization of something else. Given that Babylon is also called the great prostitute, we can assume that her abomination relates to prostitution, to sexual immorality, perhaps to an unprecedented degree.

The beast she rides has seven heads and ten horns. The angel explains that this references seven kings and then ten more. They'll unite to give power and authority to the beast who will rise to fight against the Lamb.

Pushing the evocative imagery of this passage aside, the main point is the battle between the beast and the Lamb, that is, Jesus. Don't focus on trying to discern the identity of the seven kings or the meaning of the ten who will follow. These contemplations distract us from the central theme of this passage.

The essential lesson is that Jesus, the Lamb, overcomes the attacks of the evil beast and all the power and authority given to him by Earth's kings.

Jesus will win because he is the Lord of lords and the King of kings. He stands as the supreme authority over everything on the earth. Those who follow him as his called, chosen, and faithful servants, will overcome along with him.

As such, we need not fear the assaults of the enemy, for with Jesus we will prevail.

Do we honestly believe that through Jesus we will overcome? What must we do to make sure our confidence in Jesus surpasses our fear of evil?

[Discover more about the Lord of lords in Deuteronomy 10:17, Psalm 136:3, 1 Timothy 6:15, and Revelation 19:16.]

BONUS CONTENT: IN THE SPIRIT

Then the angel carried me away in the Spirit into a wilderness. (Revelation 17:3)

The phrase *in the Spirit* (with a capital S) occurs eleven times in the Bible, all in the New Testament. John, Paul, and Peter all use this expression. This curious phrase shows up the most—four times—in Revelation.

In general, we can understand *in the Spirit* to mean not physical, not temporal, and not in (or of) this world. *In the Spirit* transcends the corporeal. It is more than a dream; it is a different reality, one which surpasses our five senses.

From a biblical perspective, consider *in the Spirit*

as a sixth sense that God supernaturally conveys to those able to perceive it.

Here are some of the scriptural uses of *in the Spirit*:

- Worship God in the Spirit and in truth (John 4:23–24)
- Praise God in the Spirit (1 Corinthians 14:16)
- Pray in the Spirit (Ephesians 6:18)
- Sharing (fellowshipping or connecting) in the Spirit (Philippians 2:1)
- Love in the Spirit (Colossians 1:8)
- Made alive in the Spirit (1 Peter 3:18)
- (Subsisting) in the Spirit (Revelation 1:10 and 4:2)
- Carried away in the Spirit (Revelation 17:3 and 21:10)

This final mention is most interesting. Though we might assume that *carried away in the Spirit* means that John's vision shows him a different location, it might be more correct to see this as a supernatural relocation of John's physical body; God translates him to another place.

We see support for this in 2 Kings 2:16 where

the prophets think God—that is, the Spirit—picked up Elijah and moved him to another location on earth. For them to hold this position would suggest that this physical translation had happened to Elijah before, or that they had known this to have occurred with others.

Another example occurs in Acts. After Philip baptizes the Ethiopian treasurer in the desert, the Spirit of the Lord takes Philip away to Azotus (Acts 8:39–40).

Another instance occurs in the expanded version of Daniel, which appears in the Apocrypha. In Judea, the prophet Habakkuk has prepared lunch for the harvesters and is on his way to deliver it. An angel appears and tells him to instead take the food to Daniel in Babylon. He's serving a seven-day sentence in a pit of hungry lions.

When Habakkuk questions God's messenger, the angel grabs him by the hair and whisks him to Daniel in Babylon. Daniel praises God for his provision and eats lunch. Then the angel returns Habakkuk to Judea (Daniel 14:28–42; sometimes called Bel and the Dragon 1:28–42.)

Throughout the Bible we see God at work *in the Spirit* in both the past and the future. We can marvel at what this means for us today.

How might we experience being in the Spirit today? How can we worship God in the Spirit and in truth?

[Read more about Elijah's story in 2 Kings 2:1–17.]

DAY 31: LEAVE HER
REVELATION 18

"'Come out of her, my people,' so that you will not share in her sins, so that you will not receive any of her plagues."
(Revelation 18:4)

I n the fight between the beast and the Lamb, we know that the Lamb is victorious. Now we hear from an angel that Babylon, the great prostitute, has fallen too. This may be because of the battle with the beast or a subsequent action. Regardless, she's been defeated. She led the nations into adultery and people prospered from her extreme extravagances.

Yet as soon as the first angel speaks, a second message arrives from heaven. It may come from

God himself. He invites the people to leave her—to come out of her—and separate themselves from her sins and the punishment they deserve from following Babylon's adulteries.

This is yet another opportunity to repent and avoid judgment.

We can speculate, without resolution, who might receive this heavenly invitation. Is it those who don't yet follow Jesus as his disciples? Is it those who received the mark of the beast, with the heavenly message offering them a final way to escape? Perhaps it's given to those who once followed Jesus but became distracted by Babylon— by the temptations of the world. If so, it's a call to return to him.

Regardless of the intended audience, we can take great solace in knowing that God gives people one more chance to repent and avoid punishment. This shows us his great mercy and immense love, wanting to save as many as he can, providing chance after chance for people to turn toward him.

Yet we also see that punishment awaits the unrepentant. This confirms God is also just.

Babylon receives a double portion of punishment. It's not just one woe, but a double woe, as in "Woe! Woe . . ." This includes torment and grief, along with plagues that produce death, mourning, and famine. Fire will consume her.

Implicitly, Babylon's punishment also awaits those who remain aligned with her depravity and refuse to turn to God.

Yet we can also receive this as a call to us today, a plea to turn from the world's distractions, represented by the great prostitute and her depravities, to leave her behind and not share in the punishment of her sins and the plagues that will afflict her.

Instead, we must realign with Jesus and escape the punishment we deserve.

How have we gotten too close to the sinful distractions of the world? What is God urging us to leave behind to return fully to him?

[Read about a parallel situation when God proclaims a double woe in Ezekiel 16:20–29.]

DAY 32: HALLELUJAH
REVELATION 19:1–10

"For the wedding of the Lamb has come, and his bride has made herself ready." (Revelation 19:7)

How many times do you think the word *hallelujah* appears in the Bible? Like me, you may have guessed many times, even hundreds. Yet *hallelujah* only shows up four times throughout all of Scripture. And they're all in this one passage in Revelation.

The first and the second *hallelujah* comes from a great multitude in heaven. Surely this mighty mass includes angels, but we don't know who else makes up this heavenly host. Regardless of who they are, they give glory to God for his judgments, for condemning the great prostitute and avenging those she martyred.

The third *hallelujah* comes from the twenty-four elders and the four living creatures. They fall prostrate and worship God, just as they've done throughout the book of Revelation. Their two-word praise is simple. "Amen," as in "may it be so" or "so be it." They follow this affirmation with a hearty "Hallelujah!"

The identity of the speakers of the fourth *hallelujah* isn't clear. John writes they sound like a huge throng, a crashing torrent, and a deafening booming thunder. They direct their praise at the Lord God Almighty. They celebrate him and give him glory.

We don't need a specific reason to praise God, because he is worthy of our adoration at any time and for any reason. Yet they're excited because the wedding of the Lamb has finally arrived and his bride—the church of Jesus—is ready.

She will dress in fine linen. It is bright and clean, which signifies the purity of a virgin. This means that when Jesus's church marries him, we will collectively stand next to him as his pure, spotless bride.

Then the angel attending to John tells him to

write that those invited to the Lamb's wedding supper are blessed. We don't know who will be in attendance to witness our wedding and partake in the wedding supper, but we do know that God esteems them as blessed.

As part of Jesus's church, what do we think about being married to him? Do we accept that through Jesus we are pure and that he views us as his wholesome, spotless bride?

[Discover more about weddings and brides in Matthew 22:1–14, John 2:1–12, and 2 Corinthians 11:2. Read more about marriage in Luke 20:27–40 and Hebrews 13:4.]

DAY 33: JESUS IS THE WORD
REVELATION 19:11–21

His name is the Word of God. (Revelation 19:13)

Though the invitations to Jesus's wedding have been sent, this doesn't mean the wedding is ready to take place. Not yet. Jesus has more to do first.

The next thing John sees in his vision is heaven opening to reveal a white horse. Mounted on the horse is a rider who is known as Faithful and True. These descriptors stand as names that reflect his character. He will act with integrity. His robe is washed in blood, which signifies success in prior battles.

The rider's name is the Word of God.

Elsewhere John wrote that Jesus is the Word and that he came to live among us (John 1:14). John also wrote that the Word was there at the beginning of time with God, and as God, at creation. Through him came light and life (John 1:1–4).

The mighty rider strikes down nations and rules them with strength. He treads the winepress, a symbol of executing judgment.

On his robe are the words, "King of kings and Lord of lords."

He is Jesus. And he's poised for battle.

The beast and the kings of the earth amass their armies to fight against the rider on the white horse and his army. Though we might expect a great confrontation, the war is short. Jesus captures the beast and the false prophet, who had convinced the people to receive the mark of the beast and worship him.

Jesus has the beast and the false prophet tossed alive into a fiery lake, burning with sulfur. Later, we will learn who will join them there and how long they'll undergo their suffering. The rest of the army dies in battle and the birds feast on their remains.

This is a gruesome end for those who oppose Jesus and his life-saving message, but it's not an outcome that those of us who follow Jesus need fear.

Our wedding with him is about to take place. The invitations have been sent. Eternal paradise awaits us—his bride, his church.

Are we, as Jesus's church, ready to marry him? Do we look forward to living for eternity with our bridegroom in paradise?

[Discover what else John says about the word of God in John 10:34–36 and 1 John 2:14. Read about the King of kings and Lord of lords in 1 Timothy 6:13–16.]

DAY 34: THE FIRST RESURRECTION
REVELATION 20

Blessed and holy are those who share in the first resurrection.
(Revelation 20:6)

With the beast and the false prophet thrown into the lake of fire, only the dragon remains. An angel comes down from heaven. He holds the key to the Abyss and carries a huge chain. He seizes the dragon, also known as the serpent, the devil, or Satan. The angel binds Satan, throws him into the abyss, locks the entrance, and seals it shut.

This will keep the beast from deceiving anyone. He'll spend one thousand years, a millennium, in the Abyss.

But remember that God views time differently than we do. To the Creator, time is relative. A thousand years to us is a day to him, and a day to us is a thousand years to him (Psalm 90:4 and 2 Peter 3:8). Regardless, Satan receives a thousand-year sentence for his crime of deception.

While Satan is bound in chains, sequestered in the Abyss, Jesus will reign. And with him others sit on their thrones, having the authority to judge. The people who will sit with Jesus are those martyred for their faith.

Specifically, they did not worship the beast or bow down to his image. They had not received his mark on their foreheads or hands. They kept themselves focused on God, worshiping him and him alone. They died for their dedication, executed for their testimony about Jesus. They paid a weighty price for what they believed in.

As a reward for their suffering, they come alive and reign with Jesus for a thousand years. They are holy and blessed, and their rebirth is the first resurrection. The second death will not affect them. And they will be priests for Father God and Jesus.

After completing his thousand-year sentence, Satan is released from his prison. He returns to doing what he did before. He deceives the nations and gathers them for battle. They march toward God's city and surround it. But before they can attack, fire shoots down from heaven and destroys them.

The devil, for his final deception, is thrown into the lake of burning sulfur. He joins the beast and the false prophet there. There they will receive everlasting torment, day and night.

With the dragon, the false prophet, and the beast (Satan) thrown into the lake of fire, it's now time for judgment to take place. We continue to move closer to the climax of our story.

But first, God sits on his throne, the great white throne. Our reality recedes from him because there's no place left for the heavens and earth to exist. The dead now stand before him and await their judgment.

The records of what they did during their life are opened and their deeds are recounted. Each one of them receives judgment for what they had done, with the guilty being thrown into the lake of fire.

How should we react to the judgment John sees in this passage? How much are we willing to give up to remain true to our faith and avoid this judgment?

[Discover more about the Abyss in its only other biblical mention in Luke 8:26–39.]

BONUS CONTENT: THE LAKE OF FIRE

Anyone whose name was not found written in the book of life was thrown into the lake of fire. (Revelation 20:15)

The dragon, the false prophet, and the beast (Satan) have been thrown into the lake of fire. John also says that death and Hades will be tossed into the lake of fire. The lake of fire is the second death. Does this mean that from this time forward death does not exist? Is dying no longer a threat to the living? Possibly. Regardless, this stands as death's final defeat.

But God consults the book of life, an account where the names of all his followers appear. It's a reassuring book that gives us comfort. We've already talked about this wonderful tome several times (Days 8 and 25, along with "Bonus Content: What Is and What Will Be").

Everyone whose name does *not* appear in the book of life is thrown into the lake of fire. Remember that this is where the dragon, false prophet, and beast remain forever, where they'll receive torment day and night. We can suspect that the same holds true for everyone who joins them there.

But everyone whose name *does* appear in the book of life will escape the lake of fire. And we excitedly await what happens next.

Do we live in confident expectation of what awaits us? How can our future hope of eternity with Jesus affect how we live today?

[Discover more about death in Isaiah 25:8 and 1 Corinthians 15:54–55. Read more about Hades in Matthew 11:23, Matthew 16:18, Luke 10:15, and Luke 16:23.]

DAY 35: A NEW HEAVEN AND A NEW EARTH

REVELATION 21:1–8

Then I saw "a new heaven and a new earth," for the first heaven and the first earth had passed away. (Revelation 21:1)

We receive John's vision of a new heaven and a new earth with much excitement. The original version, courtesy of God's creative work in Genesis 1 and 2, is no more (see Revelation 6:14.) A new heaven and a new earth await us. Remember that Jesus left the earth to go and prepare this place for us (John 14:1–4).

In this future reality exists the Holy City, the new Jerusalem. It descends from heaven to God's new Earth, prepared as a bride ready to wed her husband, Jesus the Christ. There we will live with God and God will live with us. We can imagine this might be what Adam and Eve experienced with God in the garden of Eden (Genesis 3:8) before their sin drove them from God's presence. Like them, we will walk with Father God in the cool of the day. Or it might be something even better.

This idyllic paradise is void of death, pain, and sorrow. These things are forever gone. God is making all things new. He offers living water to all who are thirsty, with no requirements or expectations. It's at no cost, a freely given gift from Jesus (Romans 5:15–18 and Ephesians 2:8–9).

Those who have overcome and are victorious, especially those who resisted worshiping the beast and taking his mark, will receive this heavenly reward as an eternal inheritance from God. And we will be his children.

Yet those who haven't aligned with God—the cowardly, the unbelieving, the vile, murderers, the sexually immoral, practitioners of magic arts, and idolaters, along with all liars—will end up forever in the fiery lake of burning sulfur. This stands as the second death, eternal damnation.

This list of negative traits gives us pause.

Though we may be able to rule out several sins we've never committed, the last item includes everyone. We have all lied at some point. Does this mean we're destined for the lake of fire? Fortunately, we are not. Through Jesus, we've been made right with God. He remembers our sins no more (Isaiah 43:25).

If we follow Jesus—if our names appear in the Lamb's book of life—we need not fear the second death. Instead, we can anticipate a joyous eternity in heaven with Jesus and Father God.

Have we accepted Jesus's freely offered gift of living water? Are we ready to receive our inheritance in God's new heaven and new earth?

[Discover more about a new heaven and a new earth in Isaiah 65:17, Isaiah 66:22, and 2 Peter 3:13. Read about living water in John 4:10–11 and John 7:38.]

DAY 36: THE BRIDE OF CHRIST
REVELATION 21:9–27

"Come, I will show you the bride, the wife of the Lamb."
(Revelation 21:9)

An angel—one of the angels who carried a bowl filled with one of the seven plagues—invites John to come with him. The messenger has something exciting to share.

The angel whisks John to a mighty mountain. From that vantage point they gaze upon the bride, the wife of the Lamb. The bride appears as the Holy City, Jerusalem, coming down from heaven and from God.

The new Jerusalem, representing the bride of Christ, shines with God's glory, a brilliance resembling the most precious of jewels. It looks like jasper, yet it is as clear as crystal.

The pair explore the new Jerusalem, the Holy City. It's a square, with walls of protection and twelve gates to allow for entry. But there's no temple. Father God and Jesus are the temple. Their glory shines bright, eliminating the need for sun or moon.

The gates remain open, yet nothing impure can ever enter. Those who have done what is shameful or deceitful will not have access. Only those who have their names written in the Lamb's book of life can enter the new Jerusalem. This means that only those whose names appear in the book of life can become the bride of Christ.

As Jesus's wife, we become children of Father God through our marriage to his Son. That's why he'll be our God and we'll be his children, his heirs.

The idea of being married to Jesus is a difficult concept for many of his followers to grasp, perhaps for men even more so than for women. The thought of a holy, marital union to the divine is enough to make most anyone squirm.

Maybe it's because no one on earth has ever seen a perfect marriage. Regardless of the love we have for our spouse or the prayerful effort we put forth to have a union that honors God and reflects his goodness, we still fall short.

Add to this that God made us male and female, husband and wife, so that we could produce children. This adds a sexual component to our human marriages. As such, we have a fleshly desire for our partners.

This image of physical desire seems inappropriate when we consider our marriage to Jesus. Yet in that context we'll have a *spiritual* desire for him, a zeal to draw close to him and be with him in a perfect union that honors our Father.

What will it be like to be the bride of Christ? How can we relate to the idea of God as our Father because of our marriage to his Son?

[Discover more about heirs of God in Romans 8:17, Ephesians 3:6, and Titus 3:4–7.]

DAY 37: TREE OF LIFE
REVELATION 22:1–5

On each side of the river stood the tree of life. (Revelation 22:2)

The angel shows John a river of the water of life, clear and pure. It springs from the throne of Father God and the Lamb. From them comes living water, the source of eternal life.

This river of living water streams down the middle of the city's main street. On each side stands the tree of life. This tree produces fruit year-round to offer sustenance and its leaves supply healing.

You may recall that the tree of life is also

present in the garden of Eden. It stands in the middle of their paradise, along with the tree of the knowledge of good and evil.

When Adam and Eve listen to the serpent's lies and disobey God, they eat from the tree of the knowledge of good and evil. In that moment they know right from wrong. Through their actions, sin enters humanity. For the first time, they realize their nakedness and are ashamed of the wonderful body God created for them. They hide from their creator.

God decides they must leave the garden, their idyllic paradise. Having already disobeyed him and eaten from the tree of the knowledge of good and evil, he fears they may also eat from the tree of life and live forever.

Though it may not seem like it at first, this reveals God's goodness. What would it be like to live forever knowing that you caused sin to enter the world? Death would serve as a release from that painful knowledge and prevent an eternity of anguish over what they did.

To spare them from everlasting agony over their sin, God expels them from the garden and assigns an angel to guard the path to the tree of life.

As they leave the garden of Eden, they leave the tree of life behind.

We don't see the tree of life again until this last chapter in the book of Revelation, the Bible's concluding passage, where it stands as a central element in the new Jerusalem. Its presence stands for eternal life in God's new heaven and new earth, an idyllic paradise where we'll live with him forever. It replaces the original Eden.

Another notable feature of this new reality that awaits us is that there will no longer be any curse. What curse? It may harken back to the first curse recorded in the Bible. It's the curse given to the serpent, Eve, and Adam for eating fruit from the forbidden tree (Genesis 3:14–19).

God now removes this curse. This doesn't matter as much to the serpent because he now lives condemned for eternity in the lake of fire. But it does matter for the curses given to Adam and Eve, which extend to their offspring, including us. These curses of pain, control, and toil, along with the eventuality of death, are no more.

What does the tree of life mean to us today? What might it be like for us not to experience the curses that God punished Adam and Eve with?

[Discover more about the tree of life in Genesis 2:9 and Genesis 3:22–24.]

BONUS CONTENT: OLD TESTAMENT IN REVELATION

"The Lord, the God who inspires the prophets, sent his angel to show his servants the things that must soon take place."
(Revelation 22:6)

Twenty verses in Revelation connect us with Old Testament passages. Nine are in the book of Isaiah. The other books are Daniel (three), Deuteronomy (one), Ezekiel (one), Hosea (one), Jeremiah (three), Psalms (five), and Zechariah (two).

Here's the list:

- Revelation 1:7 opens with a line

reminding us of Daniel 7:13 and closes with a line from Zechariah 12:10.

- Revelation 1:13 also reminds us of Daniel 7:13.
- Revelation 2:27 repeats Psalm 2:9.
- Revelation 4:8 matches Isaiah 6:3.
- Revelation 6:16 fulfills the prophecy in Hosea 10:8.
- Revelation 7:16 repeats the first part of Isaiah 49:10.
- Revelation 7:17 repeats the second part of Isaiah 49:10 and the second part of Isaiah 25:8.
- Revelation 10:9 echoes Ezekiel 3:3.
- Revelation 11:4 parallels another vision in Zechariah 4:3, 11, and 14.
- Revelation 12:5 fulfills the prophecy in Psalm 2:9.
- Revelation 13:10 repeats God's declaration in Jeremiah 15:2.
- Revelation 14:8 fulfills Isaiah 21:9.
- Revelation 14:14 echoes the vision in Daniel 7:13.
- Revelation 15:4 connects with phrases in Psalm 111:2–3, Deuteronomy 32:4,

Jeremiah 10:7, Psalm 86:9, and Psalm 98:2.

- Revelation 18:2 fulfills Isaiah 21:9.
- Revelation 18:4 repeats Jeremiah 51:45.
- Revelation 18:7 connects to Isaiah 47:7–8.
- Revelation 19:15 repeats Psalm 2:9.
- Revelation 21:1 repeats God's promise of a new heaven and a new earth from Isaiah 65:17. (This phrase also appears in 2 Peter 3:13.)
- Revelation 21:4 repeats the prophecy in Isaiah 25:8.

How can seeing John's vision scattered throughout the Old Testament enhance our view of God? How can the Bible's first mention of a new heaven and a new earth in the book of Isaiah encourage us?

[Discover more about connecting the Old and New Testaments in Luke 24:27. Read about a new heaven and a new earth in Isaiah 65:17, Isaiah 66:22, and 2 Peter 3:13.]

DAY 38: WORSHIP GOD
REVELATION 22:7–11

"Worship God!" (Revelation 22:9)

J ohn identifies himself as the author of Revelation in the opening sections of the book. In case we forgot, he reminds us that he's still here and this is his vision, which he's dutifully recording for us to read.

Overwhelmed by what he's experiencing and learning about God's new heaven and new earth, John falls at the feet of the angel to worship him. This is the second time he does this.

The first time occurred three chapters ago in Revelation 19:10. The angel chastised John and told him to stop. The heavenly being called himself a fellow servant, just like the apostle, trusting in Jesus's good news. Then the angel instructed John to "Worship God!"

You'd think John would have learned from his first attempt at angel worship. But he didn't.

Though it's a different angel this time, John again falls at his feet to worship him and pay him homage. This angel gives John the same rebuke. He tells John to not worship him since they're both servants of God. As such they should worship the Almighty.

Worship is an ongoing theme in the book of Revelation. Throughout John's vision, we see the example of the twenty-four elders and the four living creatures who sit around God's throne and devote themselves to praising him.

We also see a negative form of worship in Revelation through the people who revere the beast and receive his mark. This disrespects God. These people (along with the beast) received punishment for their misplaced worship.

These are two clear-cut examples of worship, one right and the other wrong, but John's repeated attempt at angel worship gives us a third consideration.

Though few of us would ever physically bow

down to worship anything other than God, we may effectively do this through our attitudes and our priorities. Today's world elevates sports heroes, movie stars, and politicians, placing them on a lofty pedestal. We effectively worship them through the devotion we give to them and the attention we place on their words.

They don't deserve this. They're people just like us.

We should instead worship God.

Aside from these secular examples of false worship, it also occurs within the church. We elevate ministers too, putting them on high pedestals and giving them more attention than they warrant or is wise. We admire them too much for their charisma, their ministry, and what we wrongly view as success.

We, in effect, worship them instead of the God they serve. They are just like us, servants of God who follow Jesus. May we place all our worship on the Father, Son, and Holy Spirit.

To which people do we give too much reverence at God's expense? How should we reform our worship of God to what truly honors him?

[Discover what else John writes about worship in John 4:19–24, John 9:38, Revelation 14:7, and Revelation 15:4.]

DAY 39: THE ALPHA AND OMEGA
REVELATION 22:12–16

"I am the Alpha and the Omega, the First and the Last, the Beginning and the End." (Revelation 22:13)

This passage in Revelation records Jesus's words, and it's his final teaching in the Bible. As such, it deserves our careful attention.

Jesus comes with his reward, to give each person what they deserve based on what they've done. This comes as a surprising declaration, implying that we'll receive salvation through our actions.

Aren't we saved by grace through faith? Yes, we are. Isn't salvation a gift that we can't earn? Yes, it is (Ephesians 2:8–9).

Then why will Jesus look at what we've done? Though we may remember our many sins and cringe with shame at the recollection, God blots out the sins of those who follow him, remembering them no more (Isaiah 43:25). Through him we have a clean slate.

This means that God's record of what we've done is far different than our own recollection. To him we are his pure, spotless bride (Ephesians 5:27). When we follow Jesus, we need not wallow in worry over our past mistakes because through him we are made right (Romans 5:19).

This restored standing gives us the right to eat from the tree of life. We may enter the new Jerusalem through the city gates where we'll become Jesus's bride. Nothing impure will be able to enter (Revelation 21:27).

Yet not all will have this confidence when they see Jesus coming at the end of time. He says that the practitioners of magic arts, the sexually immoral, murderers, and idolaters, along with all who persist in lying will remain on the outside looking in. He'll bar their entrance into the new Jerusalem.

Does this list sound familiar?

God gave a similar itemization in Revelation 21.

God's list is a bit longer, but he includes everything Jesus mentions. The people who do these things will end up in the fiery lake that burns with sulfur. This is the second death (Revelation 21:8).

In his message, Jesus also reveals some names for himself. He is the Root of David, as well as his Offspring, both preceding and following Israel's second king. Jesus is the bright Morning Star. And Jesus is the Alpha and the Omega. That is, he is the First and the Last, the Beginning and the End.

This is a reminder that just as Jesus is present here in Revelation at the end of time, he was also present at the beginning of creation (Genesis 1:26 and John 1:1–4). Through him we are, and through him we will be. He created our physical bodies, and he saves our spiritual selves.

Are we still holding on to the sins that Jesus has already forgiven and forgotten? How can we better respond to Jesus as the Alpha and Omega?

[Discover more about the Alpha and Omega, the First and the Last, in Revelation 1:8, 1:17, 2:8, and

21:6. Read more about the morning star in 2 Peter 1:19 and Revelation 2:28.]

BONUS CONTENT: DON'T ADD OR SUBTRACT

If anyone adds anything to them, God will add to that person the plagues described in this scroll. (Revelation 22:18)

As John wraps up the record of his vision, he tacks on a warning. He tells people to not add to his prophecy. If they do, God will give to them the plagues mentioned in this vision. And John also tells people not to remove any of his words. If they do, God will take away their share in the tree of life.

These are stern warnings which have caused me trepidation as I've written about the book of Revelation. My prayerful hope is that in explaining John's vision and sharing relevant lessons for us today, I have not inadvertently added to or subtracted from John's work. I fear many others have done so, either by piling their own interpretations upon John's vision or diminishing what it means or even ignoring it completely.

I have also been concerned by preachers who take this warning out of context. Instead of applying it only to John's vision, as he says to do, they apply it to the entirety of Scripture, even though the New Testament as we know it didn't exist when John recorded his vision.

In their viewpoint they criticize others for adding content (often called the Apocrypha) to the Bible. However, the books of the Apocrypha were part of the Septuagint, which was in wide use during Jesus's time, and he quoted from it. Furthermore, the books of the Apocrypha were also in the original King James Version of the Bible, but these books were later *removed*. One explanation is that we only have Greek versions of this text available to us today and none in Hebrew.

If anyone deserves criticism, it's those who removed these books from the Bible.

What must we do to make sure we don't take Bible passages out of context? How can we fully embrace all of God's Word?

[Discover more about God's Word in 2 Timothy 3:16–17.]

DAY 40: COMING SOON
REVELATION 22:17–21

He who testifies to these things says, "Yes, I am coming soon." (Revelation 22:20)

After Jesus finishes his last teaching, the Holy Spirit weighs in as well. But it's not just him. It's also the bride (not the bridegroom). This means you and me, all whose names appear in the Lamb's book of life. We join with the Holy Spirit to bid people to "Come!" And everyone who hears our offer we'll add to the invitation and likewise say to others, "Come!"

This invite is to anyone who's thirsty. They may come to him. Anyone who wants to can receive

Jesus's no-strings-attached gift of living water. Isn't this exciting?

Only a few verses ago, in Revelation 22:11, it seemed too late for those who hadn't already decided to follow Jesus. But now it feels as though they're given one last, final chance. The invitation, given three times, is to come to Jesus and receive the water of life.

We serve a God of second chances. And third chances. And even more than we can count. He is patient because he wants as many to come to him as possible (2 Peter 3:9).

But we need to come to Jesus before it's too late, perhaps before he returns, which will happen soon.

In this chapter in Revelation, Jesus speaks three times.

The first is in verse 7. Then comes his longer message (which we just covered) in verses 12 through 16. His final words in all of Scripture appear at the end of verse 20.

In each of these three passages he repeats the same phrase: "I am coming soon."

This threefold testimony from Jesus that he's coming soon repeats to underscore its importance. Though Jesus saying it once is enough, saying it twice adds emphasis, while three times confirms beyond all doubt that it will happen.

Yet we must acknowledge that God reckons time differently than we do. What is *soon* to him may not be *soon* to us. Indeed, 2,000 years ago Jesus told his followers that his kingdom was near, that it was coming soon. The early church understood this as meaning any day, just as many people now make the same assumption.

As Jesus's followers, how can we understand his promise that he is coming soon? How should we live our lives in this tension between him coming soon and having already waited two millennia?

We must embrace both scenarios.

We should strive to simultaneously expect that he's coming back today and seek to live every day for the rest of our lives to advance his kingdom and raise up future generations to follow him too. We should balance the seemingly competing realities that he is coming soon *and* that we may die before he does.

Since Jesus could come any day, what are we doing to make each remaining moment count? And as we wait, what are we doing to produce a long-term kingdom impact?

[Discover more about Jesus coming soon in Hebrews 10:36–37, Revelation 2:16, and Revelation 3:11. Read about the kingdom of God (heaven) being near in Matthew 3:2, Mark 1:15, and Luke 21:31.]

If you liked *Revelation Bible Study*, please leave a review online. Your review will help others discover this book and encourage them to read it too.

Thank you.

HOW TO HAVE YOUR NAME WRITTEN IN THE LAMB'S BOOK OF LIFE

Many people read the book of Revelation and tremble with foreboding over what is to come. Indeed, for those who don't know Jesus, whose names aren't in the Lamb's book of life, there's much to fear over what they will encounter and the second death that will result, where they'll spend the rest of eternity in the burning lake of fire.

Yet for those whose names are written in the Lamb's book of life, Revelation fills us with awe about what is to come. We can navigate the end of time with the confidence that God will protect us in whatever difficulties we face. We know we'll spend the rest of eternity with him in the new heaven and new earth that he'll create for us. What a glorious time that will be.

We all want to be sure our name appears in the Lamb's book of life, the record of those who will spend eternity with Jesus.

A recurring theme in the Bible's four biographies of Jesus is people asking him what they must do to receive this eternal life, that is, to enter the kingdom of God/heaven, to receive salvation, to be saved.

What's frustrating is that Jesus doesn't always give the same answer. He tells different people to do various things. But regardless of the specifics, each individual instruction reduces to one specific aim: follow Jesus.

Much of the time, Jesus simply says, "Follow me" or "Repent and follow me."

To repent means to make a U-turn. That is, to stop what we're doing and choose an alternate route, to do something different. When we follow Jesus, we choose a different path. We make a U-turn in our life. We repent—we stop what we're doing—and go all in for him. We follow him and become his disciples.

When we do this, Jesus enters our name in his book of life. Then we can face the end times with confidence because we know what awaits us.

Thank you, Jesus.

If your name is in the Lamb's book of life, what can you do to show Jesus your appreciation? And if your name isn't yet in the Lamb's book of life, will you begin following Jesus today?

[Discover more about salvation through Jesus in Acts 4:12, Romans 10:13, Ephesians 2:8–9, Philippians 2:12–13, 1 Thessalonians 5:8–9, Titus 2:11, Hebrews 9:27–28, 1 Peter 1:3–12, and 1 Peter 2:2, as well as throughout the entire Bible.]

FOR SMALL GROUPS, SUNDAY SCHOOL, AND CLASSROOMS

Revelation Bible Study makes an ideal eight-week Bible study discussion guide for small groups, Sunday School, and classrooms. In preparation for the conversation, read one chapter of this book each weekday, Monday through Friday.

- Week 1: read 1 through 5.
- Week 2: read 6 through 10.
- Week 3: read 11 through 15.
- Week 4: read 16 through 20.
- Week 5: read 21 through 25.
- Week 6: read 26 through 30.
- Week 7: read 31 through 35.
- Week 8: read 36 through 40.

When you get together, discuss the questions at the end of each chapter. The leader can use all the questions to guide this discussion or pick which ones to focus on.

Before beginning the discussion, pray as a group. Ask for Holy Spirit insight and clarity.

As you consider each chapter's questions:

- Look for how this can grow your understanding of the Bible.
- Evaluate how this can expand your faith perspective.
- Consider what you need to change in how you live your lives.

End by asking God to help apply what you've learned.

May God bless you as your read and study his word.

IF YOU'RE NEW TO THE BIBLE

Each entry in this book contains Bible references. These can guide you if you want to learn more. If you're not familiar with the Bible, here's an overview to get you started, give some context, and minimize confusion.

First, the Bible is a collection of works written by various authors over several centuries. Think of the Bible as a diverse anthology of godly communication. It contains historical accounts, poetry, songs, letters of instruction and encouragement, messages from God sent through his representatives, and prophecies.

Most versions of the Bible have sixty-six books grouped into two sections: The Old Testament and the New Testament. The Old Testament contains thirty-nine books that precede and anticipate Jesus. The New Testament includes twenty-seven books and covers Jesus's life and the work of his followers.

The reference notations in the Bible, such as Romans 3:23, are analogous to line numbers in a Shakespearean play. They serve as a study aid. Since the Bible is much longer and more complex than a play, its reference notations are more involved.

As already mentioned, the Bible is an amalgam of books, or sections, such as Genesis, Psalms, or 1 Peter. These are the names given to them, over time, based on the piece's author, audience, or purpose.

In the 1200s, each book was divided into chapters, such as Acts 2 or Psalm 23. In the 1500s, the chapters were further subdivided into verses, such as John 3:16. Let's use this as an example.

The name of the book (John) appears first, followed by the chapter number (3), a colon, and then the verse number (16). Sometimes called a chapter-verse reference notation, this helps people quickly find a specific text regardless of their version of the Bible.

Although the goal was to place these chapter and verse divisions at logical breaks, they sometimes seem arbitrary. Therefore, it's good practice to read what precedes and follows each passage you're studying. The text before or after it may contain relevant insights into the portion you're exploring.

Here's how to look up a specific passage in the Bible based on its reference: Most Bibles contain a table of contents, which gives the page number for the beginning of each book. Start there. Locate the book you want to read, and turn to that page. Then flip forward to the chapter you want. Last, skim that chapter to locate the specific verse.

If you want to read online, enter the reference into BibleGateway.com or BibleHub.com. Also check out the YouVersion app.

Learn more about the greatest book ever written at ABibleADay.com, which provides a Bible blog, summaries of the books of the Bible, a dictionary of Bible terms, Bible reading plans, and other resources.

ABOUT PETER DEHAAN

Peter DeHaan, PhD, wants to change the world one word at a time. His books and blog posts discuss God, the Bible, and church, geared toward spiritual seekers and church dropouts. Many people feel church has let them down, and Peter seeks to encourage them as they search for a place to belong.

But he's not afraid to ask tough questions or make religious people squirm. He's not trying to be provocative. Instead, he seeks truth, even if it makes people uncomfortable. Peter urges Christians to push past the status quo and reexamine how they practice their faith in every part of their lives.

Peter earned his doctorate, awarded with high distinction, from Trinity College of the Bible and Theological Seminary. He lives with his wife in beautiful Southwest Michigan and wrangles crossword puzzles in his spare time.

A lifelong student of Scripture, Peter wrote the 1,000-page website ABibleADay.com to encourage people to explore the Bible, the greatest book ever written. His popular blog, at PeterDeHaan.com, addresses biblical Christianity to build a faith that matters.

Read his blog, receive his newsletter, and learn more at PeterDeHaan.com.

BOOKS BY PETER DEHAAN

For the latest list of all Peter's books, go to PeterDeHaan.com/books.

40-Day Bible Study Series

Dear Theophilus (the Gospel of Luke, formerly That You May Know)

Dear Theophilus, Acts (formerly Tongues of Fire)

Dear Theophilus, Isaiah (formerly For Unto Us)

Dear Theophilus, Minor Prophets (formerly Return to Me)

Dear Theophilus, Job (formerly I Hope in Him)

Living Water (the Gospel of John)

Love Is Patient (Paul's letters to the Corinthians)

Revelation Bible Study

Love One Another (John's letters)

Run with Perseverance (the book of Hebrews)

James and Jude Bible Study

Matthew Bible Study

1 & 2 Peter Bible Study (coming in 2025)

Mark Bible Study (coming in 2025)

Holiday Celebration Bible Study Series

The Advent of Jesus (an Advent devotional)

The Passion of Jesus (a Lenten devotional)

The Victory of Jesus (an Easter devotional)

The Ministry of Jesus (an Ordinary Time devotional)

Bible Character Sketches Series

Women of the Bible

The Friends and Foes of Jesus

Old Testament Sinners and Saints

More Old Testament Sinners and Saints

Heroes and Heavies of the Apocrypha

Visiting Churches Series

Shopping for Church

Visiting Online Church

52 Churches

The 52 Churches Workbook

More Than 52 Churches

The More Than 52 Churches Workbook

Other Books

Jesus's Broken Church

Martin Luther's 95 Theses

The Christian Church's LGBTQ Failure

Bridging the Sacred-Secular Divide

Beyond Psalm 150

How Big Is Your Tent?